THE EXTRAORDINARY BOOK OF

USELESS
INFORMATION

THE EXTRAORDINARY BOOK OF

Useless Information

*The Most Fascinating Facts
That Don't Really Matter*

DON VOORHEES

A PERIGEE BOOK

A PERIGEE BOOK
Published by the Penguin Group
Penguin Group (USA)
375 Hudson Street, New York, New York 10014, USA

USA I Canada I UK I Ireland I Australia I New Zealand I India I South Africa I China

Penguin Books Ltd., Registered Offices: 80 Strand, London WC2R 0RL, England
For more information about the Penguin Group, visit penguin.com.

Library of Congress Cataloging-in-Publication Data

Voorhees, Don.
The extraordinary book of useless information : the most fascinating facts that
don't really matter / Don Voorhees. — First edition.
pages   cm
ISBN 978-0-399-16517-7
1. Questions and answers.   I. Title.
AG195.V645   2013
031.02—dc23   2013017463

First edition: September 2013

PRINTED IN THE UNITED STATES OF AMERICA

10 9 8 7 6 5 4 3 2 1

ALWAYS LEARNING   PEARSON

To all my loyal readers
who enjoy useless information as much as I do.
Enjoy!

CONTENTS

MASCOT MUSINGS

There are 1.8 million squirrel hunters in the United States.

Squirrels will dig up crack cocaine buried by drug dealers/addicts, eat it, and become quite aggressive.

Sugar Bush Squirrel is an eastern gray squirrel that was rescued by one Kelly Foxton and now is featured on its own website (sugarbushsquirrel.com) appearing in photos wearing one of three thousand custom-made little outfits and posed with various props.

Female red squirrels will mate with up to fourteen different males a day when in heat.

In 2012, a bright purple squirrel was captured in Jersey Shore, Pennsylvania. Scientists were unable to explain its bizarre coloring.

Marmots, which are really large ground-dwelling squirrels, now leave hibernation earlier in the Rocky Mountains and are getting fatter, due to global warming.

Twice in one week, a flying squirrel invaded the emergency room at Robert Wood Johnson University Medical Center in New Brunswick, New Jersey.

Paleontologists have discovered the fossilized remains of a 100-million-year-old saber-toothed squirrel in Argentina.

Squirrels in California have been found that carry the plague.

Just in time for Christmas, one enterprising company is now selling freeze-dried squirrel's feet earrings.

BODY SHOP

OH BABY!

Babies can't taste salt until they are between two and six months old.

Infants have taste buds all over the insides of their mouths, not just on the tongue.

A protein called, appropriately enough, noggin delays the plates in a baby's skull from fusing together until the baby reaches the age of six months.

A baby born in 2011 has a 50 percent chance of living to be one hundred, according to current estimates.

Babies born in the autumn have a better statistical chance of living a long life.

The most popular day for a baby to be born is Tuesday, followed by Monday. Sunday is the slowest day in that regard.

The most babies are born in September, followed by August, June, and July.

An infant loses much more heat through its head than an adult, which accounts for those caps put on babies in hospital maternity wards. An adult loses about 10 percent of body heat through the head.

New studies have found that "third-hand" smoke, found in clothing, is a danger for young children's brain development.

One in ten women report having smoked during pregnancy.

Scientists suspect that about one in eight pregnancies are multiples at the very beginning, but one fetus dies early and is never detected. This is known as a "vanishing twin."

Fetuses can regrow almost any body part damaged in the womb and children under two have been known to regrow fingertips.

THE EYES OF BABES

At the age of six months, babies stop fixating on other people's eyes and begin watching their mouths to figure out, by lip reading, how to make the sounds of speech. By age one year, most babies have figured this out and go back to paying more attention to the eyes of others.

THAT SUCKS

Newborn boys have been known to die from disseminated herpes simplex virus Type I after undergoing the ultra-Orthodox Jewish circumcision ritual called *metzitzah b'peh*, where the rabbi (mohel) removes the blood from the penis using his mouth.

LADIES' ROOM

The longer a woman's labor is, the greater the likelihood that she will have a boy.

The more pregnancies that a woman has, the greater the chance that she will develop gum disease.

Cells from a human fetus can migrate into the mother's brain and stay there for years.

A 2012 study found that men whose mothers had high blood pressure during their pregnancy tend to score lower on IQ tests than those whose mothers had normal blood pressure levels.

In the last three decades, the average woman's foot has gone from a size seven and a half to a size eight and a half or nine.

At the turn of the twentieth century, the average woman wore a size four shoe. From the forties to the sixties, five and a half was the average.

Roughly 87 percent of American women have had foot problems from wearing ill-fitting or uncomfortable shoes, such as high heels.

An increasingly popular surgical procedure for women is having their toes shortened, or even having their pinky toes removed, to make wearing stilettos and sandals easier.

In general, women tend to increase their alcohol consumption after getting married. Men tend to drink less.

Men are 1.5 times more likely to get Parkinson's disease than women. Ladies seem to be protected somewhat by the female hormone estrogen.

Men are also three times more likely than women to get hepatocellular carcinoma, the most prevalent type of liver cancer.

WIVES WITH HIVES

Some women are allergic to their partner's semen. These unfortunate ladies suffer from seminal plasma hypersensitivity, which causes hives, tissue inflammation, and in the worst cases, death. Some twenty to forty thousand American women are affected.

Even stranger, some men are allergic to their *own* semen. These men will show allergic symptoms around their eyes and nose and flu-like symptoms shortly after climaxing. Sufferers can be cured through hyposensitization therapy, where they are injected over time with ever-increasing doses of the allergen—namely their own semen.

Some women suffer from autoimmune progesterone dermatitis. They break out in hives after ovulation each month due to a hypersensitivity to progesterone.

Cold urticaria sufferers develop redness, itching, and hives after exposure to cold. Cold air, cold water, and cold drinks can trigger a reaction. Swimming in cold water can cause a full body reaction that may cause lowered blood pressure, fainting, shock, and even death.

In 2001, a nineteen-year-old man died from cardiopulmonary arrest after eating pancakes made from a box of mix that had been opened two years earlier. Apparently the man was highly allergic to a mold that had grown in the mix.

9,400,000 American children suffer from skin allergies, and 3,443,000 suffer from food allergies.

Kids from wealthy families are more likely to suffer from peanut allergies than less affluent children.

PARASITE POWER

Before the twentieth century, autoimmune diseases, such as Crohn's, multiple sclerosis, and type 1 diabetes, were virtually nonexistent. This is because people bathed and washed very infrequently years ago, and all that filth activated an immune response. Today's hygienic practices remove parasites that the immune system was designed to attack, and it attacks itself instead. This is why these diseases are much less prevalent in less-developed countries today.

Scientists are now using therapies where microscopic worms and their eggs are ingested by those suffering from Crohn's, celiac disease, and ulcerative colitis to reset the immune system, preventing it from attacking itself.

THAT MAKES SENSE

The front, back, and sides of the tongue have most of the taste buds. The middle has virtually no taste sensation.

Humans have more pain nerve endings than any other type of nerve ending.

The least sensitive spot on the body is the middle of the back.

According to some researchers, humans recognize seven primary smells—camphoraceous (mothballs), ethereal (dry-cleaning fluid), musky (perfume), pepperminty, pungent (vinegar), putrid (rotten eggs), and roses (floral).

Some blind people can use echolocation, in much the same manner as some animals, to orientate themselves and determine the shapes and sizes of objects by using clicking sounds made with the tongue or tapping a cane on the ground.

> One notable practitioner of echolocation was Ben Underwood, who had both his eyes removed at age three, but was able to skateboard, ride a bike, and play basketball.

Scientists have recently found that humans can actually smell fear and disgust in others, and that these emotions are contagious. Researchers collected the sweat of men viewing scary or disgusting movies and had women then smell said perspiration. The ladies sniffing the "scary" sweat opened their eyes wide in a frightened reaction and those getting a whiff of the "disgusting" sweat scrunched up their faces in revulsion.

> Women generally are more sensitive to smells than are men.

GOLDILOCKS

The Melanesians, who inhabit the islands north and east of Australia, are the only dark-skinned people to have blond hair.

The single genetic mutation that causes blond hair in European populations occurred about eleven thousand years ago. Before this there were no blond Europeans.

It is estimated that approximately one-third of adult white American and European females dye their hair some shade of blond.

WHAT CAN BROWN DO FOR YOU?

Doctors now can transfer the feces of a healthy person into the colon of a person suffering from colitis. The procedure, known as fecal microbiota transplantation, involves processing the healthy poop into a smooth puree that is infused into the patient via an enema or colonoscopy tube. The healthy fecal microbes displace the bad microbes, alleviating the problem.

WHAT AILS YOU

The average healthy person has about ten thousand different germ species living in and on his or her body.

All the microbes in a human body, taken together, weigh about three pounds.

More than twelve thousand different diseases are known to affect humans.

The plague originated in Mongolia when soil-dwelling bacteria mutated into killing machines.

Plague still kills about three thousand people a year worldwide.

The seasonal flu shot is only 62 percent effective at preventing influenza—not enough to prevent a global outbreak.

Smallpox in the United States was eradicated in 1949, polio in 1979, measles in 2000, and rubella in 2004.

Polio has been eradicated in every country in the world except Afghanistan, Nigeria, and Pakistan, where it is endemic.

2011 saw the most deadly known outbreak of food-borne illness in history. An unusually virulent strain of *E. coli* bacteria found in fenugreek seeds, used to make sprouts, sickened more than four thousand people and killed at least fifty.

Going out in the cold with wet hair or feet does *not* increase one's chances of catching a cold or flu.

The first diagnosed cause of cancer occurred in 1775, when a British doctor noticed a high rate of scrotal cancer in chimney sweeps.

One-half of all men and one-third of all women develop some type of cancer during their lifetime.

A study has found that tanning bed use is responsible for 170,000 skin cancer cases a year. The International

Agency for Research on Cancer lists ultraviolet radiation from tanning beds as a Class 1 carcinogen, the same category as tobacco smoke and asbestos.

THE BIG FREEZE

People who suffer from migraine headaches are more likely to get brain freeze.

HO-HUM

Contagious yawning occurs at a faster rate among friends and family than among strangers.

NOW EAR THIS

Scientists can now grow a replacement ear on someone's arm and transplant it to their head.

Australian artist Stelarc has implanted a third ear beneath the skin of his arm. He plans to attach a microphone to the ear once it has fully grown in and wirelessly link the device to the Internet so others can listen in.

CURIOUS CONDITIONS

Epidermolysis bullosa (junctional EB) is a rare disease that causes the skin to blister at the slightest movement. Babies born with the disease lack the protein needed to hold the inner and outer skin layers together, resulting in friction between the layers and blistering. The blisters are usually worst around the eyes and in the mouth. Life expectancy for such children is about one year.

A Memphis, Tennessee, woman suffers from a mystery illness that causes human nails to grow from her hair follicles. She contracted the condition after an allergic reaction to steroids.

A Las Vegas man who suffers from scrotal elephantiasis has a scrotum that weighs one hundred pounds. He carries around a plastic milk crate to support his massive testicles. Doctors have no idea what caused this condition and castration may be the only solution.

Professional commercial voice-over man Tom Rohe lost his voice after having a wisdom tooth removed. Rohe, whose career was ruined, found that his speech returned whenever he took the sleep aid Ambien. He now takes low doses to be able to speak, but his voice is not back to its former professional quality.

A condition known as rapid eye movement sleep behavior disorder causes sufferers to act out their dreams while asleep. Kicking, punching, jumping, and screaming are common causes of injury that may result.

Sultan Kösen of Turkey is the tallest man the world. He suffered from acromegaly, a tumor on the pituitary gland that caused him to grow to a height of eight feet, three inches before surgery curtailed his continued growth in 2010.

Adam Rainer is the only documented person who was both a dwarf *and* a giant. Born in Austria-Hungary, Rainer was just four feet tall at age eighteen. Due to what is believed to have been a pituitary tumor, he had shot up to seven feet, eight inches by the time of his death at age fifty-one.

Congenital insensitivity to pain afflicts about one hundred Americans. Sufferers have a normal sense of touch and can feel hot, cold, and tickling, but feel no pain.

The artificial butter flavoring used in microwave popcorn can be hazardous to one's health. Diacetyl, used as a flavoring in the late 2000s, caused the respiratory disease bronchiolitis obliterans, also known as popcorn lung, in workers with long-term exposure to the chemical. A Colorado man who had eaten microwave popcorn twice a day for ten years won a $7.2 million lawsuit when he was diagnosed with popcorn lung.

Porphyria is a condition that may cause the skin to blister and the feces and urine to turn purple when exposed to light, as well as other symptoms. *Porphyra* means "purple pigment" in Greek.

Large joint arthropathy can cause the joints to turn black, as well as the whites of the eyes and the earlobes.

Brainerd diarrhea is a sudden onset of explosive, watery diarrhea that lasts for months or years. Only time will cure this condition. It was first documented in Brainerd, Minnesota, in 1983.

In rare cases, tumors called limbal dermoids, which produce hair, have been known to grow on the eyeball.

People who have haemolacria cry tears of blood. This condition can have many causes, but is most prevalent in menstruating women and may be induced by the hormone estrogen.

Nodding disease affects children in East Africa, causing permanently stunted growth and seizures that cause the head to nod. These seizures are brought on by eating or by feeling cold. Even the sight of food can bring on nodding. Once the child stops eating or is warmed up, they cease. Curiously, the eating of unfamiliar foods does not bring on seizures.

Jumping Frenchmen of Maine is a rare disorder first found in northern Maine among French Canadian lumberjacks. It causes sufferers to have a heightened startle reflex, which makes them jump at the slightest stimuli. They also are very prone to suggestion, obeying commands given suddenly and imitating the actions of those around them.

In 1962, an outbreak of mass hysteria known as the Tanganyika laughter epidemic occurred. Schoolgirls began having uncontrollable bouts of laughter that lasted from a few hours to sixteen days. Other symptoms included flatulence, crying, screaming, fainting, and rashes. Overall, one thousand people were affected and fourteen schools had to be shut down.

Equally odd was the Dancing Plague of 1518 in Strasbourg, France. In a month's time, some four hundred people began dancing uncontrollably for days at a time. Many died from exhaustion, heart attacks, and strokes.

The 1983 West Bank fainting epidemic affected nearly one thousand Palestinian schoolgirls. The wave of dizziness, nausea, headaches, and fainting forced the closing of West Bank schools for twenty days. It is believed mass hysteria was the cause, after false rumors of poisoning were circulated.

A 1997 episode of *Pokémon* aired on Japanese TV caused hundreds of people, mostly school age children, to go into seizures. The convulsions, fainting, and nausea started just after a five-second scene depicted flashing red lights in the eyes of the character Pikachu.

WHAT'S LEFT?

Left-handed people are more likely to suffer from dyslexia, schizophrenia, and ADHD than are righties.

High stress during pregnancy results in an increased chance of having a left-handed baby, as does low birth weight.

In some identical twins, one is right-handed and one is left-handed.

Left-handed people on average earn less money.

One percent of the population is ambidextrous.

THAT'S THE SPIRIT

In 1895, Anheuser-Busch sold Malt-Nutrine, a 1.9 percent alcohol beer that doctors could prescribe as a nutritional supplement for children.

Whiskey and brandy were listed as medicines in the *United States Pharmacopeia* until 1916.

Muscle tissue, which absorbs alcohol more effectively than fat tissue, prevents more of it from reaching the brain, meaning fat people are likely to get tipsy quicker than more muscular folks.

A recent study suggests that, in general, wine drinkers are rather unadventurous, while vodka drinkers like to be in charge, and tequila drinkers are free-spirited.

SUPER-SIZE ME

The posting of calorie contents on fast-food menus makes no difference in the amount people eat.

A recent study found that girls who eat frequent meals and snacks put on fewer pounds and gain fewer inches on their waistlines than those who only eat a couple of times a day, probably because the frequent meals and snacks keep them satisfied and prevent them from overeating.

People who eat moderate amounts of chocolate regularly are thinner than those who eat it less often.

Severe obesity is 50 percent higher among women than among men and twice as high among blacks as among Hispanics and whites.

RAIN MEN

Steven Wiltshire is a British architectural artist who is also an autistic savant and can precisely draw the exact arrangements and sizes of the buildings of a city from memory, right down to the windows, after one look. In 2009, after a twenty-minute helicopter ride around Manhattan, he rendered from memory a precise eighteen-foot-long drawing of the New York metropolitan area.

Kim Peek, the inspiration for the movie *Rain Man*, had memorized twelve thousand books verbatim by the time of his death in 2009. He could also rattle off the zip code, area code, TV stations available, and highways for any town in the United States. It is believed he suffered from a rare genetic disorder known as FG Syndrome.

Wim Hof of the Netherlands is impervious to cold. Through Tummo Tantric Buddhist meditation he is able to control his autonomic nervous system so that he can maintain his body temperature after being submerged in an ice bath for over an hour. He once tried to climb Mount Everest wearing only a pair of shorts, but failed due to a foot injury.

OUT COLD

Sleeping in a cold room can cause bad dreams.

BODY OF KNOWLEDGE

The hardest bone in the body is the jawbone.

A fully inflated human heart has an internal surface area of one hundred square yards.

It's impossible to talk while inhaling through the nose.

The eyes always see the nose, but the brain simply chooses to ignore it.

The liver has at least five hundred different functions.

Whispering puts more strain on the vocal cords than does speaking normally.

The wrinkling of the skin on fingers and toes when exposed to water for a prolonged time may be an evolutionary adaptation to increase grip in wet conditions.

THE PINOCCHIO EFFECT

New research claims that when a person lies, the temperature of the skin around the person's nose increases.

STICKY PROBLEM

Each year, 1.5 million Americans are injured by medical tape removal. Newborns and the elderly are the most easily injured, and permanent scars can result.

ATTACK OF THE QUACKS

Dr. Henry Cotton was an American psychiatrist who ran the state mental hospital in Trenton, New Jersey, from 1907 to 1930. Cotton believed that mental illness was the result of untreated infections in the body, and therefore had his staff remove patients' teeth, which harbored germs. If this "cure" did not work, he progressively had the tonsils, cervix, testicles, ovaries, gall bladder, stomach, spleen, and colon removed, depending on which organs he felt were "infected." Cotton gained international praise for his "progressive" work. He even had some of his own teeth removed after suffering a nervous breakdown. Sadly, up to 45 percent of his patients died from surgical complications.

In 1998, British doctor Andrew Wakefield published a paper linking childhood vaccines to autism, sparking one of the worst health scares ever. Countless parents refused to have their kids vaccinated, and many still do today, even though Wakefield was totally discredited and found to have ties to class action trial lawyers, who cashed in on the scare. He had his medical license revoked, and no subsequent study has shown any linkage between vaccines and autism.

Deaths in teaching hospitals spike 10 percent in July. This is when the new doctors start their first year of residency.

It's Not Rocket Science

GIDDY UP

Horsepower is technically defined as the amount of power required to lift 33,000 pounds by one foot in one minute. By this definition, the average horse only boasts 0.7 horsepower.

Early cars had a radiator cap on the top front of the hood with a temperature gauge known as a "motometer." When temperature gauges moved to the dashboard, hood ornaments replaced them. Large hood ornaments were given the heave-ho in the 1950s, as they were deemed dangerous to pedestrians in collisions.

GERM OF AN IDEA

There are an estimated 1 billion microbial species on Earth.

The germiest thing commonly touched in public places is the handle of a gas pump. Seventy-one percent of pumps tested were covered in nasty bacteria, such as *E. coli* and *Salmonella*. The next two germiest things are escalator rails and ATM buttons.

Bacteriophages (phages) are viruses that attack bacteria.

Phages are the most abundant form of life on Earth.

Phages were used to treat bacterial infections before the discovery of antibiotics and are still widely used for that purpose today in Eastern Europe.

Bacteriophages are sprayed on ready-to-eat meats to kill *Listeria*.

The oldest living thing may have been a bacteria sample taken from Siberian permafrost that survived for 400,000 to 600,000 years.

NO SEX, NO PROBLEM

Bdelloid rotifers are tiny creatures that live in water. They are asexual, but oddly have developed quite a genetic diversity over the past 80 million years for a creature that does not swap DNA through sex with other rotifers. Uniquely, scientists believe they acquire new DNA from the bacteria, algae, and fungi they ingest.

UNDER PRESSURE

The pressure created by the carbon dioxide in a bottle of champagne is ninety pounds per square inch.

> The Armstrong line, or limit, is the altitude (about twelve miles) at which the atmospheric pressure is so low that exposed bodily fluids, such as tears, saliva, and fluid in the lungs, will boil away at normal human body temperature. Above this height, pressurized suits or cabins are required.

Daredevil Felix Baumgartner was the first person to have skydived from above the Armstrong line, plummeting twenty-four miles. He reached a top speed of 834 miles per hour during his four-minute-nineteen-second free fall.

WHAT A BLAST

The world's most powerful laser is in the National Ignition Facility at Lawrence Livermore National Laboratory in Livermore, California. It can produce blasts with 500 trillion watts, more power than the entire United States uses at any instant in time. Because the blasts last just five-millionths of a second, they only consume about twenty dollars' worth of energy a pop.

> The estimated temperature at the moment of the Big Bang was 100 million trillion trillion degrees Kelvin.

The average temperature on Earth today is 288 degrees Kelvin.

ANTICIPATION

Researchers at MIT have invented a coating for plastic bottles that is so slippery that every last bit of ketchup will flow right out of the container.

YOU ARE WHAT YOU EAT

Carbon monoxide is injected into plastic-wrapped meat packaging to prevent oxidation, which will cause red meat to turn brown.

Castoreum is a yellowish secretion from the castor sacs found near the tails of beavers mixed with their urine. Castoreum is used as a "natural" raspberry, strawberry, or vanilla flavoring in some foods and drinks and also adds flavor and aroma to some cigarettes.

Common sand is used in salts, coffee creamers, and soups to prevent clumping.

Ground marble is used as a coating on chewing gums.

Propylene glycol, which is found in antifreeze, is used in sodas, beer, and salad dressings to help ingredients mix better.

Ground up South American cochineal beetles are used as a red coloring in several different foods, such as Yoplait yogurts, Kellogg's Pop-Tarts, and Starbucks Strawberries and Cream Frappuccino mix.

Scientists have engineered a cow that gives milk free of beta-lactoglobulin, the protein that triggers milk allergies.

Adding oil to boiling pasta does not keep it from sticking together since the oil floats atop the water and doesn't come into contact with the pasta until it is drained, and then it makes it difficult for the sauce to adhere. Oil is added to the water to keep it from boiling over.

There is no conclusive scientific evidence that MSG causes or worsens migraine headaches.

A 2011 investigation by *Consumer Reports* found that 10 percent of apple juice tested had dangerously high levels of inorganic arsenic, a carcinogen, and 25 percent of apple juice was found to have unsafe levels of lead. Eighty-eight brands were tested.

FATAL FARTS

A new British scientific study has calculated that the dinosaurs may have become extinct from their own gas emissions (that is, their farts), not from an asteroid strike. An estimated 520 million tons of methane gas a year were produced by the giant beasts, enough to cause global warming and their own demise.

VIVE LA FRANCE

In 1852, Frenchman Henri Giffard created the first powered aircraft when he outfitted a hydrogen-filled dirigible (balloon) with a three-horsepower steam engine.

The names of seventy-two renowned French scientists, engineers, and others of distinction are engraved around the outside of the Eiffel Tower, just below the first balcony.

THE GREAT UNKNOWN

A 2011 census of world species found that they number close to 8.7 million, excluding bacteria. There are 5,500 mammal species on Earth.

There are an estimated 750,000 marine species that have yet to be discovered and described, approximately three times the number that have already been described.

DUCK TAPE

Duct tape is not good for taping ducts. It tends to quickly dry out and fall apart when used for such a purpose. The product was probably originally known as "duck" tape when it debuted in World War II, for sealing ammunition boxes.

WORTH ITS WEIGHT IN GOLD

A gallon of water weighs 8.3 pounds. The same volume of gold weighs 160.9 pounds.

CREEPY CONTINENTS

The continents of North and South America are slowly creeping northward, as are Asia and Europe. It is estimated that they will collide in about 100 million years, closing the Arctic Ocean and the Caribbean Sea.

CARBON FOOTPRINT

Odor-Eaters insoles are made with activated carbon.

Activated carbon is made by heating coconut shells to a very high temperature, which causes the powder to become riddled with microscopic pores.

One gram of activated carbon has a surface area equal to that of a football field, making it is the most adsorbent substance in the world.

IN THE GREEN

Three-quarters of the oxygen in the atmosphere is produced by algae in the oceans.

A large oceanic algal bloom can cover a greater surface area than the Amazon rain forest.

A well-watered golf fairway will require 1.6 million gallons of water a year.

THE OCEAN BLUE

The surf near San Diego, California, periodically lights up like a neon glow stick as it crashes onto the beach. This phenomenon is caused by phytoplankton in the water that are bioluminescent and emit an eerie blue light when disturbed. Surfers and swimmers splashing in the water also cause the strange light show to occur.

CHANNEL SURFING

The first remote control was invented in the 1920s. It was used to control a radio and had a dial like an old phone.

In the late 1950s, Zenith came out with ultrasound remotes for their TVs that changed the channels using ultrasonic (high-frequency sound) waves. Today's remotes use infrared light.

A LITTLE LEARY

William Lear, who is best known for founding the Learjet Corporation, also invented the first car radio and the 8-track audio cartridge tape. He developed them for use in his private jets.

FREAKS AND GEEKS

Some people "sleep text," sending incoherent text messages to family and friends while asleep. They have no recollection of doing so upon awakening.

Engineering students spend the most time studying—nineteen hours per week on average. By comparison, business and social science majors average fourteen hours per week of study time.

THIS JUST IN . . .

A 2010 University of Indiana study found that men pay more attention to the nightly newscast when an attractive woman is delivering it, but are less likely to remember what she said, as compared to when an unattractive female or a male newscaster reads the news.

Women were found to be more attentive to a newscast when an attractive man delivered it, but in contrast to the male viewers, they had no problem remembering what the newscasters said.

YOU'VE GOT MAIL

Perhaps the person with the most recognizable voice who no one has ever heard of is Elwood Edwards, who is the voice of the AOL messages "Welcome" and "You've Got Mail."

Musician Brian Eno, who wrote the start-up music for Microsoft Windows 95, known as the Microsoft Sound, did so on an Apple Mac computer. Eno later said that he had never used a PC because he does not like them.

NO SWEAT

The relative humidity level at which perspiration fails to evaporate from the skin is about 60 percent.

Gore-Tex, which was patented in 1976, was invented by Wilbert Gore, his son Robert, and Rowena Taylor. The fabric allows water vapor (perspiration) to pass through, but not water droplets (rain). This is how it keeps the wearer dry.

INNOVATION STATION

A Japanese laboratory has invented a "Kiss Transmission Device" that consists of a plastic straw that when wiggled with the tongue will transmit a signal to another such device and remotely make its straw wiggle, presumably while in another's mouth.

Other Japanese inventors have come up with an air bladder–filled vest that will compress to simulate being hugged, in lieu of an actual hug from another person.

The Lifesaver water filtration bottle, invented by Brit Michael Pritchard, is the size of a standard liter water bottle and contains a nano-filtration hollow fiber membrane that removes bacteria and viruses from the dirtiest water. One filter can purify six thousand liters of water.

German biochemist and fashion designer Anke Domaske has invented a new fabric made entirely from milk. Marketed under the trade name QMilch, it drapes like silk and can be washed like cotton. Made from strands of milk protein, the fabric is said to be ideal for those with very sensitive skin and is more ecologically friendly than traditional fabrics.

In 2011, the world's smallest electric motor was created by Tufts University chemist Charles Sykes. It consists of a single molecule. The carbon and hydrogen atoms that stick out from it make the molecule spin like a propeller when an electrical charge is focused on it by a scanning tunneling microscope. The rotating molecule can then cause surrounding molecules to spin, acting like mechanical gears.

The strongest insect repellent ever was invented in 2011. It is 100,000 times more effective than DEET (the most commonly used insect repellent). The compound, known as VUAA1, is also cheaper and longer-lasting than DEET. It works by overstimulating a bug's olfactory system so that it cannot smell humans, or anything else.

In 2011, scientists at MIT developed the fastest camera system ever, capable of recording 1 trillion exposures per second. The camera is so fast that it can render a light beam moving in slow motion.

The darkest substance known to science is made from carbon nanotubes that are stacked and sandwiched together. This material absorbs 99.9 percent of the light that hits it. The microscopic surface is rough and uneven, making it a very poor reflector, and its superconductive properties also help it absorb light.

HOT STUFF

Chlorine trifluoride is the most flammable chemical. It will combust on contact with almost anything and burns such materials as asbestos, concrete, glass, sand, and flame retardants.

WEIRD SCIENCE

The world's lowest density solid, Aerogel, also known as frozen smoke, is a silicon gel with all the liquid taken out and replaced with gas, making it 96 percent air. When a piece is held in the hand, it is almost impossible to feel or see. Aerogel can support four thousand times its own weight and is the best insulator known to man.

Gömböc is the world's only self-righting object. Developed in 2005, it is shaped in such a way that no matter how it is put down, it will always stand itself back up. Unlike Weebles, which self-right because of a weight in the bottom, Gömböc does so simply because of its shape. It has since been found that turtles share the same basic shape, allowing them to easily right themselves.

Gallium is a silvery metallic element that melts at 85°F. Crystals of this metal are on the market, and one can hold a gallium crystal in one's hand and watch it slowly melt into a shiny puddle that will freeze back into a solid when it cools.

Oobleck is a suspension of starch (such as cornstarch) in water and is an example of a non-Newtonian fluid (a liquid that does not behave as a typical liquid). Although it is a fluid, it becomes solid when pressure is applied to it. As such, a person can run across a vat of liquid oobleck.

Chilled caramel is another non-Newtonian liquid. Caramel on top of ice cream is a liquid, but if a finger is pushed rapidly into it, the caramel acts like a solid. A spoon pushed slowly in will keep the caramel in its liquid state, but pulling the spoon out quickly will cause it to form a solid. The same effect can be achieved by turning a container holding chilled caramel upside down rapidly.

EcoSpheres are sealed glass balls of seawater, algae, bacteria, and shrimp. These tiny ecosystems will live for years. All they require is warmth and sunlight.

DISHWASHER DISCOVERIES

Fish can be steamed in a dishwasher. To do so, wrap fish tightly in aluminum foil and run on the normal cycle with no detergent. Do not run the dry cycle. Enjoy.

Lemonade-flavored Kool-Aid can be used to remove iron and lime stains from a dishwasher. Simply empty a packet in the detergent dispenser and run the dishwasher.

LOTTO LOWDOWN

Studies show that people play lottery numbers 31 and down more often than higher numbers, probably because many bettors play birthdays.

BLOWIN' IN THE WIND

Tumbleweeds are not native to the American West, but originated in Eurasia.

Tumbleweeds are unique in that they disperse their seeds by rolling across the ground when blown by the wind.

A LITTLE NIBBLE

A "nibble," in computing, is four bits, or half a byte. It is also spelled "nybble" and "nyble."

PINHEAD NUMBER

The most common ATM PIN number is 1234. These incredibly unimaginative four digits make up 10.7 percent of PIN numbers. 1111 is second, with a user frequency rate of 6 percent. 0000, 1212, and 7777 round out the top five most popular PINs.

IN THE PINK

The color magenta gets its name from the dye magenta that was discovered shortly after the Battle of Magenta in 1859, near Magenta, Italy.

WATTS UP?

A one-watt night-light emits a billion billion photons per second.

PLANE AND SIMPLE

Flying in an airplane is safer than riding an escalator.

About 97.5 percent of passengers involved in a fatal plane crash survive.

Statistically speaking, a person would have to fly every day for thirty-five thousand years to be in a fatal plane crash.

The safest places to sit on a plane are in the back or in the middle over the wing.

The black box and flight recorders are kept in the tails of planes because that is the section most likely to survive a wreck.

PLASTIC IS FOREVER

Each year the United States uses about 102 billion plastic grocery bags.

Plastic molecules are too big for bacteria and fungi to break down. Sunlight, however, does degrade plastic, making it brittle and causing it to fracture into tiny pieces.

THAT BLOWS

Hurricane Alice has the distinction of being both the earliest *and* latest hurricane on record. It began on December 30, 1954 and ended on January 5, 1955. No other hurricanes have been active so late in a year, or so early in a year.

The only years on record in which there were no Atlantic hurricanes were 1907 and 1914.

IN A FOG

The foggiest place in the world is the Grand Banks off of Newfoundland, where the warm waters of the Gulf Stream meet the cold waters of the Labrador Current.

The foggiest place in the United States is Point Reyes, California, which averages more than two hundred foggy days a year.

Redwood trees in California receive 30 to 40 percent of their moisture from fog.

Precipitation that falls from a cloud but evaporates before it reaches the ground is called virga.

Cloudy nights are warmer than clear nights, since clouds trap heat absorbed by the Earth during the day, preventing it from being lost back to space when the sun goes down.

Helicopters are sometimes used to clear fog from the runways at airports.

WEATHER UPDATE

Raindrops are not tear-shaped, but actually resemble mushroom caps.

The last snowfall of the season is known as the onion snow.

The warmest it has ever been in Antarctica was 59°F at Vanda Station on January 5, 1974.

SPACED OUT

Astronauts report that space has a distinctive odor. Upon returning from a spacewalk, their spacesuits have a metallic smell, similar to that of seared steak or welding fumes.

Bacteria grow faster in space.

Water in space boils in one big bubble, instead of the thousands of tiny ones found in earthbound boiling water.

Candle flames in space are spherical, not tear-shaped.

Many astronauts who spend too much time in space begin to develop blurry vision. Scientists aren't sure why this happens, but it could complicate efforts to send people on long-term missions, such as to Mars.

The first person to walk in space was Soviet cosmonaut Alexey Leonov, in 1965. His spacesuit was not properly pressurized and it ballooned and stiffened so much that Leonov got stuck trying to reenter the space capsule's air lock after first entering it the wrong way. He had to reduce the pressure in his suit to free himself, and he risked death from the bends.

Astronauts' urine is discharged into space. Their feces are brought back to Earth. The astronauts who landed on the moon left all their trash, including excrement, behind for future visitors to find. Apollo astronauts pooped into a bag and then had the odious task of squirting in some germicide and kneading the contents to sterilize said poop.

Many early space shots involved sending live animals into orbit. Sadly, none of these dogs, apes, and other animals ever returned safely to Earth. In fact, dozens of them are still orbiting the planet in mummified form.

STARSTRUCK

The sun is really a white star. It is the Earth's atmosphere that makes it appear yellow.

Most stars are smaller than the sun and most have a companion star.

The sun is closest to the Earth in early January.

The seasons on Earth have nothing to do with its distance from the sun, but with the tilt of the Earth's axis.

Brown dwarfs are space objects that are bigger than large gas planets (like Jupiter) but smaller than stars. Some brown dwarfs are as cool as 80°F.

Newly discovered stars, known as Y dwarfs, are about the size of Jupiter and are almost cool enough to touch. They remain so cool because their size is too small to allow fusion to take place. One of the nearest stars to Earth is a Y dwarf. Brown dwarfs that cool off become Y dwarfs.

VY Canis Majoris is the largest known star, some two thousand times the size of the sun. It is so big that it would take a jet plane twelve hundred years to fly around it.

A marshmallow dropped on a neutron star would impact with the force of an atomic bomb due to the star's enormous gravity.

There are so many stars at the center of the Milky Way Galaxy that if the Earth were moved there, there would be 1 million stars in the sky and there would be no night.

A recent study of the cosmos suggests that the universe is running out of star-making material and that new star formation is coming to an end.

Scientists now believe there are at least 176 billion galaxies in the universe.

The Hubble Space Telescope can see galaxies oneten-billionth as bright as the naked eye can see.

The farthest away galaxy was discovered/photographed in 2011. Named GN-108036, this galaxy is believed to be

12.9 billion years old, just 750 million years younger than the universe itself.

If the sun was replaced by a black hole of equal mass, the orbits of the planets would not be affected.

Once a black hole forms, it never dissipates.

FRANKENSTORM

There was a massive storm on Saturn in 2011 that stretched some two hundred thousand miles, with a vortex nearly as wide as Earth.

STARDUST

Comet dust contains the gemstone peridot.

GREAT BALLS OF FIRE

Meteoroids that are large enough to impact the Earth are called meteorites.

Most meteoroids visible in the night sky are at an altitude of forty to seventy-five miles above the Earth.

Sometimes the sonic booms created by meteoroids can be heard on the ground. During the 2001 Leonid meteor shower, people reported hearing a cracking sound.

EARTH SCIENCE

If Earth didn't have an atmosphere, the sky would always be black, as on the moon. The atmosphere scatters sunlight, making it look blue.

Four billion years ago, an Earth day was just ten hours long. Tidal friction, or gravitational force, between the Earth and the moon has slowed Earth's rotation over the years. It is currently slowing at the rate of twenty seconds every million years.

Parts of Canada near the Hudson Bay have less gravity than the rest of the world.

Earthquake lights are multicolored lights, similar to aurorae, that appear in the sky during earthquakes and volcanic eruptions.

GREAT MINDS

Isaac Newton wrote more about his Bible interpretations and the occult than he did about science.

Modern scholars believe Newton may have had Asperger's syndrome.

Biographers speculate that Newton, who never married, may have died a virgin.

Galileo Galilei was an excellent lute player.

Galileo's middle finger is on display at the Museo Galileo in Florence, Italy.

Francis Bacon died after contracting pneumonia while studying the effects of freezing on the preservation of meat—perhaps bacon.

Bacon married a fourteen-year-old girl when he was forty-five.

Charles Darwin married his first cousin. Whenever one of their children would get sick, he worried that it was because of inherited weakness due to inbreeding with his cousin.

Charles Francis Richter, of Richter scale fame, was an avid nudist.

Greek mathematician Pythagorus did not discover the Pythagorean theorem—$a^2 + b^2 = c^2$. It was known to the Babylonians some time earlier.

EASY AS PI

Pi is the ratio of a circle's circumference to its diameter. Its decimal representation never ends and never repeats. Pi, in short, is roughly 3.14159.

Computers have calculated pi to more than ten trillion digits.

In 2005, a Chinese man named Lu Chao set the world record for reciting the digits of pi, correctly rattling off pi to 67,890 digits in just over twenty-four hours.

PAPER MOON

If an ordinary one-millimeter-thick sheet of paper could be folded 42 times, it would reach past the moon. Folding it 51 times would make it extend out past the sun. Folding it 60 times would reach past the edge of the solar system. Folding it 83 times would make it thicker than the diameter of the Milky Way Galaxy, and unbelievably, folding it 103 times would put it near the edge of the known universe! (Each time the paper is folded, it doubles the previous thickness, resulting in phenomenal growth. This is the power of exponential math!)

ICE, ICE, BABY!

Depending on temperature and pressure, there are fifteen known "phases" of ice. All ice found in the biosphere is known as Ice I. The different kinds of ice differ in their density and crystalline structure.

It is believed that under high enough pressures, ice may become a metal.

SLIME TIME

Slime molds are giant one-celled organisms with many nuclei that may be up to several square feet in size.

Even though they have no brain, slime molds have the ability to "remember" where they have been. They lay down a trail of goo as they slide along and use its presence to retrace their path or move in a new direction.

That musty odor of old books is caused by the spores of the fungi that live on the pages. Some experts believe that breathing the spores of some of these fungi for a period of time can cause hallucinations.

SIZING YOU UP

That gadget they use to measure your feet at the shoe store is known as a Brannock Device.

BIG BIRD

Sixty-seven million years ago, a giant flying pterosaur the size of an F-16 fighter jet, named *Quetzalcoatlus*, lived in what now is Texas.

SPORTS PAGE

LET THE GAMES BEGIN

The 1900 Olympics had a live pigeon shooting event.

The 1904 Games had club swinging, an event that involved the twirling of clubs.

The 1924 Games had an event called La Canne, a French sport similar to fencing, that used wooden canes.

Rope climbing was an Olympic event up until 1932.

World Olympic record-holder South Korean archer Im Dong-hyun is legally blind, with 10 percent vision in one eye and 20 percent in the other. He does not wear glasses or contacts during competition.

Olympic gold medals are only 1.34 percent gold. The rest is comprised of 93 percent silver and 6 percent copper. The metals in the gold medal are worth about $650, as of 2012.

Olympic silver medals are comprised of 93 percent silver and 7 percent copper.

Bronze medals are mostly copper.

A study of Olympic medalists found that they live an average of 2.8 years longer than members of the general public.

In 2012, Olympic swimmer Michael Phelps sunk the longest televised putt in history when he holed a 159-footer at the Dunhill Links Championship in Scotland. The putt took seventeen seconds to reach the cup. Phelps had only been golfing seriously for two months before accomplishing the feat.

American William Fiske won Olympic gold in the bobsled in the 1928 and 1932 Winter Games. He was just sixteen years old in the 1928 Games and was the flag bearer in the 1932 Games. Fiske also holds the distinction of being the first American killed in World War II. He pretended to be a Canadian and joined the British RAF in 1940, before the United States entered the war. He died in the Battle of Britain.

The U.S. Olympic flag bearer is selected by a vote of the captains of the various sports represented.

ISN'T IT IRONIC?

Chaunté *Lowe* is an American high jumper who competed in the 2012 Olympics.

Sylvia *Fowles* is an American basketball player who competed in the 2012 Olympics.

BAD SPORTS

The only gold medal won by Ireland in the 2004 Olympic Games came in show jumping. Unfortunately the winning horse—Waterford Crystal—tested positive for a performance-enhancing drug and was stripped of the medal.

At the 2008 Olympic Games, Cuban tae kwon do athlete Angel Matos was disqualified during a match after he took a longer than allowed injury time-out. He responded by kicking the referee in the face.

In his fencing match, Russian pentathlete Boris Onishchenko used an electronically rigged dueling sword that automatically scored hits, whether he touched his opponent or not. He was disqualified.

DON'T QUIT YOUR DAY JOB

Most American Olympic athletes work normal jobs and train in their spare time. Some examples from the 2012 team are triathlete Gwen Jorgensen, who is an accountant; discus thrower Lance Brooks, who is a construction worker in the oil business; sailor Debbie Capozzi, who works in the family Italian ice shop; and wrestler Chas Betts, who works as a motions designer (graphic arts) for films and videos.

American Suzy Favor-Hamilton, who ran in the 1992, 1996, and 2000 Summer Games, supplemented her income as a high-priced call girl, earning up to six hundred dollars per client.

TO DIE FOR

Hall of Fame baseball player Ed Delahanty died in 1903 after a conductor kicked him off a train for being drunk and disorderly. Delahanty then attempted to walk over the International Railway Bridge connecting Buffalo, New York, to Fort Erie, Ontario, and either jumped or fell into the Niagara River and was swept over the falls.

Formula One racer Alan Stacey was killed during the 1960 Belgium Gran Prix after a bird hit him in the face, causing him to crash.

In 1998, an entire soccer team was killed by lightning during a match in the Democratic Republic of the Congo. The opposing team was fine.

In 1983, Dick Wertheim, a tennis official at the U.S. Open, died after player Stefan Edberg hit a ball into his crotch, causing Wertheim to fall over and hit his head on the court.

MULTIPURPOSE MAN

On September 8, 1965, Bert Campaneris of the Oakland A's became the first major-league baseball player to play all nine positions in a single game. On the mound, he pitched ambidextrously, throwing lefty to left-handed batters and righty to right-handers. Since then, three more players have accomplished the feat.

AROUND THE HORN

Johan Santana became the first Mets pitcher ever to throw a no-hitter, in 2012. The only problem was that the umpire called a ball hit down the third base line foul, when replays clearly showed it to be fair.

In 2012, a baseball jersey worn by Babe Ruth circa 1920 sold for $4.4 million. That topped the previous record holder for sports memorabilia—the original rules for the game of basketball written by James Naismith—which sold for $4.3 million in 2010.

Mickey Mantle of the New York Yankees holds the record for most home runs in World Series history with eighteen. He is followed by Babe Ruth with fifteen, Yogi Berra with twelve, Duke Snider with eleven, and Lou Gehrig and Reggie Jackson with ten.

The average major-league baseball salary in 1967 was $6,000. The average salary in 2012 was $3.2 million.

FOOTBALL RULES

About 36 percent of Americans say pro football is their favorite sport, followed by college football and pro baseball at 15 percent each, and auto racing at 8 percent.

The NFL's online store reported that Green Bay quarterback Aaron Rodgers had the top-selling jersey for the 2011 season, followed by Denver Broncos quarterback Tim Tebow and Pittsburgh Steelers safety Troy Polamalu. Teamwise, the Steelers sold the most jerseys.

Purdue quarterback Drew Brees threw the most passes in an FBS college football game—eighty-three—against Wisconsin in 1998. He completed fifty-five of them. Despite the pass-happy Brees, Purdue lost the game 31–24.

In 2012, forty-two college football coaches earned at least $2 million a year.

According to *Forbes* magazine, the most valuable college football program in the United States is the Texas Longhorns, followed by Notre Dame, Penn State, Louisiana State University, Michigan, Alabama, Georgia, Arkansas, Auburn, and Oklahoma.

Lehigh University and Lafayette College have the longest-running rivalry in college football, 148 games and counting, as of 2012. The series began in 1884, with the only interruption occurring in 1896.

The Michigan football team holds the record for consecutive games without being shut out—349. The next four are Florida at 297, TCU at 242, Air Force at 233, and Tennessee at 222.

Since its inception in 1935, only three teams have had back-to-back Heisman Trophy winners. Larry Kelley (end) and Clint Frank (halfback) won for Yale in 1936 and 1937. Doc Blanchard (fullback) and Glenn Davis (halfback) won for Army in 1945 and 1946. Matt Leinart (quarterback) and Reggie Bush (running back) won for USC in 2004 and 2005. (In 2010, Bush became the first winner to forfeit the award.)

ZEBRAS

Black-and-white stripes first appeared on football officials' uniforms in the 1920s, after a quarterback in a college game tried to hand the ball off to an official in an all-white shirt.

Officials in the old American Football League wore red-and-orange-striped jerseys.

There are seven officials for an NFL game. They are the head referee, umpire, head linesman, line judge, side judge, back judge, and field judge.

The referee is the crew chief and wears a white hat, while the other officials wear black ones. He stands behind the offense and watches for penalties involving the quarterback or running back. The referee is the final authority on the field and is the one who communicates game information directly to the crowd via a wireless microphone. He also confers with the replay official in a booth above the field on instant replay challenges.

The umpire stands behind the defensive line and linebackers and watches for offensive holding and illegal forward passes. He is also responsible for making sure the players' equipment is legal.

The head linesman stands on one side of the field at the line of scrimmage. He looks for offsides penalties and determines if a player steps out of bounds. The head linesman also is in charge of the first down chain crew and marks forward progress on the field.

The line judge stands on the opposite sideline from the head linesman and also watches for offsides and out-of-bounds. In addition, he keeps track of the time during the game as a backup to the clock operator.

The field judge stands behind the defensive secondary, on the same side of the field as the line judge. He determines pass interference, pass completions, and illegal blocks downfield, and rules on whether field goal attempts are successful.

The side judge has the same responsibilities as the line judge, but on the opposite side of the field.

The back judge works the middle of the field behind the defensive secondary. He watches for pass interference, pass completions, illegal blocks downfield, and delay of game penalties.

NFL officials first started announcing penalties to the crowd in 1975.

NFL officials make about nine thousand dollars a game.

IT TAKES A LOT OF BALLS

In an NFL football game, the home team provides thirty-six new balls for an outdoor game and twenty-four balls for one played indoors. There are an additional twelve balls supplied for the kickers. The referee checks the air pressure in the balls prior to kickoff.

KICKER'S KORNER

Statistics show that "icing" a kicker—that is, the opposing coach calling a time-out just before a kicker attempts a high-pressure field goal—makes no difference. However, when the Dallas Cowboys inexplicably iced their own kicker in a 2011 game against the Cardinals, he missed the game-winning field goal, after making it just before the time-out.

The longest high school field goal was sixty-eight yards. Dirk Borgognone of Reno, Nevada, accomplished the feat in 1985. The NFL record is only sixty-three yards.

Kickers make 99.3 percent of extra points attempted in the NFL.

BACKWARDS BARRY

Barry Sanders holds the NFL record for most carries by a running back for negative yardage—336. These plays resulted in minus 952 yards.

In a 1994 playoff game against the Green Bay Packers, Sanders had a grand total of minus one yards rushing on thirteen carries.

MANNING UP

New York Giants quarterback Eli Manning's full name is Elisha Nelson Manning. He was named after his father, Elisha Archibald "Archie" Manning III, who was also a star NFL quarterback.

Eli's older brother's full name is Peyton Williams Manning.

Cooper Manning is the eldest Manning brother. He was a Mississippi all-state wide receiver who was thought to have a bright future in football, until he was diagnosed with spinal stenosis (a narrowing of the spinal column) at the age of eighteen.

As of late November 2012, the Manning family has thrown a combined 750 NFL touchdown passes—Peyton (425), Eli (200), and Archie (125).

CHEAT SHEETS

The first professional quarterback to use a wristband with the plays written on it was Tom Matte of the Baltimore Colts in 1965. Matte was actually a running back on the team, but was forced to play QB after injuries to Johnny Unitas and his backup, Gary Cuozzo.

THE WONDERLIC YEARS

The year future NFL football prospects are eligible for the draft, they are given something called the Wonderlic test to determine their intelligence. It is a fifty-question SAT-like exam that must be completed in twelve minutes. One point is awarded for each correct answer. The average score is 20.4. Historically, centers have the highest average score (26), followed by quarterbacks (25), offensive tackles (22.5), offensive guards and tight ends (22), safeties and linebackers (21), defensive ends (20), defensive tackles and fullbacks (19), receivers and cornerbacks (18), and running backs (17).

PASSING MUSTARD

The lowest passer efficiency rating in the NFL is 0.0. To achieve such a distinction, a quarterback must attempt at least ten passes, have a completion percentage of 30 percent or less with no touchdowns, average fewer than three yards per attempt, and have an interception percentage of 9.5 percent or higher.

> Four-time Super Bowl winner Terry Bradshaw holds the record with a zero quarterback rating in a game three times. Joe Namath did it twice and Johnny Unitas once.

The highest passer rating possible in the NFL is 158.3. To achieve such a rating, a quarterback must attempt a least ten passes, have a completion percentage of at least 77.5 percent, an 11.875 touchdown percentage, a minimum of 12.5 yards per pass attempt, and no interceptions. Thirty-five different quarterbacks have achieved this rating in a game since the advent of the system in 1973. Peyton Manning has had four perfect games; Ben Roethlisberger and Kurt Warner have thrown three.

> Ex–NFL quarterback Donovan McNabb and NFL defensive end Julius Peppers are the only two people to have played in a Super Bowl and an NCAA Final Four basketball game. McNabb was a reserve on the 1996 Syracuse basketball team that lost to Kentucky in the Final. He also lost in his only Super Bowl appearance. Peppers was a reserve on the 2000 University of North Carolina basketball team that lost to Florida in the Final Four semifinals, and he lost in his only Super Bowl.

POUTY PATRIOT

Those weird-looking logos on either side of the field in Gillette Stadium, the home of the New England Patriots, are stylized representations of the bridge and tower found at the north end of the stadium.

The midfield logo in Gillette Stadium is a stylized patriot, known locally as "flying Elvis" because of his long sideburns and pouty expression.

GO SKINS

In the eighteen presidential elections that have taken place since the Washington Redskins moved to Washington in 1937, seventeen have been predicted by the team's performance in its final home game before the election. If the Redskins win, the incumbent does also.

WHAT'S THE PUNCH LINE?

The 1944–45 Montreal Canadiens hockey lineup of Rocket Richard, Elmer Lach, and Toe Blake, known as the "Punch Line," were 1-2-3 in the National Hockey League in scoring that season.

Carolina Hurricanes goalie Cam Ward scored a goal without touching the puck. According to NHL rules, the last player to touch the puck gets credit for the next goal scored by his team. Ward stopped a goal by the attacking New Jersey Devils near the end of a game on December 26, 2011. The Devils, who had pulled their goalie from the net to insert another attacker, inadvertently sent the puck back into their own goal on an errant pass. Ward was credited with the score since he was the last Hurricane to touch the puck.

BIRDIES OF A FEATHER

Traditional badminton shuttlecocks, or birdies, were made from about sixteen overlapping feathers from the left wing of a goose or duck.

WEARING THE YELLOW JERSEY

Professional cyclists in long races, like the Tour de France, will pee off to the side while riding their bikes. The trick is not to spray the riders to the rear while doing so.

*BAD*SKETBALL

Kobe Bryant's wife Vanessa got half of the couple's $150 million assets when they divorced due to allegations of Bryant's infidelity. She also got three mansions in the Newport Beach, California, area, one of which her mother lives in.

In more bad basketball news, a judge garnished Allen Iverson's bank account to put toward $375,000 worth of jewelry the former star never paid for. Iverson made about $150 million in his career.

Star NBA basketball player Tony Parker cheated on his wife, actress Eva Longoria, with the wife of his San Antonio Spurs teammate Brent Barry. Both couples subsequently divorced.

In 1997, Charles Barkley was arrested for throwing a man through an Orlando, Florida, nightclub's plate glass window after the man had thrown a glass of ice at Barkley.

Barkley has confessed to having lost about $10 million on gambling, $2.5 million of it during one particularly poor six-hour blackjack session.

FUTILITY FACTOR

In 2012, the Portland Trailblazers set an NBA record for missing all twenty of their 3-point shot attempts in a 92–74 win over the Toronto Raptors.

WILLIAMS TO WILLIAMS TO WILLIAMS TO WILLIAMS

The 2011 New Jersey Nets NBA basketball team had four players with the last name Williams. They sometimes were all on the court at the same time during a game, making it quite challenging for the play-by-play announcers.

NBA player Ron Artest changed his name to Metta World Peace.

HOOP SCOOP

On November 20, 2012, Jack Taylor, who was a sopho-more player on the Grinnell College basketball team in Iowa, shattered the NCAA scoring record by pouring in 138 points in a regulation game. He took 108 shots, made 27 of 71 three-pointers, averaged one shot every twenty seconds, and scored four points a minute in the second half. A player on opposing Faith Baptist Bible scored sev-enty points and they still lost by seventy-five points. Tay-lor's best effort before this game was forty-eight points when he was in high school.

DISPOSABLE INCOME

In 2012, Tiger Woods's ex-wife, Elin Nordegren, bought a $12-million mansion in Florida and promptly had it demolished to make room for an even more expen-sive one.

MARATHON MAN

American ultramarathon runner Dean Karnazes once ran fifty marathons in fifty states in fifty days.

FLIP-FLOPPER

In 2012, American Keith Levasseur ran the Baltimore Marathon in a time of 2:46:58 while wearing flip-flops.

WILD THINGS

SLEEPY TIME

Opossums sleep twenty hours a day.

> Walruses have air sacs beneath their throats that they inflate to keep their heads above water while sleeping at sea.

Migrating thrushes will land briefly to take micro-naps lasting only eight seconds.

HIDING IN PLAIN SIGHT

A "new" species of frog has been discovered in the most unlikely of places—the New York metropolitan area. It went unnoticed for so long because it closely resembles the local southern leopard frog that lives in the region.

> In 2010, a new species of bee was discovered in New York City. The blue-green, non-stinging sweat bee, about the size of a sesame seed, licks salt from sweaty people.

There are about 250 native bee species found in New York City, the highest number of any major city.

Half of the world's spider species have yet to be discovered.

MONKEY BUSINESS

The first new monkey species discovery in twenty-eight years was confirmed in the Democratic Republic of the Congo in 2012. The golden-maned primate is known as a lesula.

Black howler monkeys in an Argentine natural park were treated with antidepressants after two of the elder females in the group died.

Male chimpanzees have spines on their penises that can injure the female during mating.

GOING APE

Bonobos, chimpanzee-like apes that live in the Congo, have sex more than any other primate. They do so several times a day, with multiple partners, in multiple positions, regardless of gender or age.

Bonobos are the only nonhuman primates to engage in tongue kissing and oral sex.

Bonobo society is matriarchal, with females ruling. They use sex to keep the males in line.

A bonobo mother will carry and nurse her young for four years.

FOR THE BIRDS

The expression "crazy as a loon" comes from the fact that the common loon's call sounds like the wild laughter of a demented person.

The name "loon" comes from the Swedish *lom*, meaning "lame." This waterfowl's feet are set so far back on its body that it has difficulty walking on land.

Woodpeckers have barbed tongues so that they can grab insects out of the holes they peck in trees.

Bald eagles return to the same stick-built nest each year, adding to its size annually. Some older nests can weigh up to one thousand pounds.

The golden eagle is North America's largest predatory bird.

A barn swallow's nest consists of one thousand beakfuls of mud.

American kestrels are able to see ultraviolet (UV) light. This enables them to locate rodents by their urine, which glows bright yellow in UV light.

Great horned owls can hear a mouse moving beneath a foot of snow.

Great horned owls lay their eggs in January or February.

The curious name of the titmouse comes from the Scandinavian word *tit*, meaning "little," and the Old English word *mase*, meaning "bird."

The tufted titmouse will pull the fur from sleeping cats and dogs to line its nest.

Robins do not cock their heads to listen for worms. They hunt by sight, and their eyes are set so far back on their heads that they must tip their heads to one side to see the ground.

Swifts spend all their daylight hours on the wing, never perching. They drink by dipping into water, and they collect twigs by snapping them off while in flight.

Barn swallows may fly up to six hundred miles a day in search of food for their young.

Some male marsh harriers grow female plumage to protect these transvestite birds from other males.

Birds have better color vision than do humans. While humans have three color cones in their eyes—red, green, and blue—birds have a fourth type—violet.

In Stockholm, Sweden, the pigeons hitch a ride on a local subway instead of flying. From their resting area the birds take the train one stop to their preferred feeding site near a mall that has plenty of cafes and Dumpsters for their dining pleasure.

More than 250 bird species engage in a behavior known as anting, where they rub dead insects, usually ants, on their feathers. It is thought that the chemicals in the bugs acts to kill parasites on the birds, and the oils found in the insects may supplement the bird's own natural oils.

Emperor penguins can dive to depths of 1,750 feet in search of food.

Only five of the seventeen penguin species live in cold climates.

"I TAWT I TAW A PUDDY TAT!"

Feral cats rival window strikes as the main killers of birds.

According to the U.S. Department of the Interior's *State of the Birds* report, domestic and feral cats kill hundreds of millions of birds each year and are one of the reasons that one-third of America's eight hundred bird species are endangered, threatened, or in serious decline.

The caracal is a cat found in Africa and Western Asia that can jump ten feet into the air from a crouching position, to grab birds in flight.

JUST DUCKY

Ducks maintain a constant body temperature of 105° F, even in the coldest winter.

The blood flowing to a duck's feet is cooled first so that there is no loss of body heat when swimming in frigid waters.

Ducks have an oil gland on their backside that they use to waterproof their feathers while preening.

The common eiger duck eats whole mollusks, shells and all. The duck's gizzard grinds up the shells, and the calcium they contain finds its way into future eggshells.

Ducks are one of the only birds in which males may forcibly copulate with unreceptive females if they can't find another mate.

Ducks have antibiotics in their sperm that fight off sexual diseases in males and females. The brighter a male duck's bill is, the stronger the antibiotics in his sperm.

LET'S TALK TURKEY

Male turkeys keep harems of up to twenty females.

Turkeys roost in trees at night.

CAT COUNTRY

A cheetah can spot a rabbit from two miles away.

The cheetah is the only cat that does not have retractable claws.

Cheetahs are one of the only cats to hunt during the day.

The binturong, also called the bearcat, is an animal from Southeast Asia that looks like a cross between a bear and a cat. It is unique in that it smells just like hot, buttered popcorn.

The palm civet, which is a relative of the binturong, can kill a cobra by running around it in circles until the snake becomes dizzy and falls over, at which point the feisty little mammal strikes.

SOMETHING'S FISHY

The snakehead is an introduced fish from Asia and Africa that invaded Maryland in 2002 and is now in seven states. Known locally as the "fish from Hell," it can live for four days on dry land and can travel a quarter mile between bodies of water.

There are electric catfish in Africa that are capable of producing a 350-volt shock to incapacitate their prey.

Clownfish live in groups of up to six members around a single anemone. The largest and most dominant fish is always a female. The next in size is the male, and the other four smaller fish are immature, without gender. Once the immature clownfish do develop a gender, they can change their sex if one member of the mating pair dies.

A female brown trout will fake orgasms to trick males into releasing their sperm, while she does not release her eggs. This behavior causes undesirable males to leave her alone so she can find a more suitable mate.

Fish can taste with their fins and tail.

Ten thousand sea rays migrate from the waters off the Yucatán Peninsula to the coast of Florida in spring and back again in fall.

The heart of a blue whale measures nine feet across and weighs about one ton.

The spade-toothed whale is the rarest and most reclusive whale in the world. It is also probably the least understood large mammal. Two specimens that washed up on a beach in New Zealand in 2010 are the only ones ever found. The creature has never been observed in the wild. Its existence had only been conjectured from a partial jawbone found in 1872 and skull bones found in the 1950s and 1986.

Dolphins hear at least ten times better than people.

The Chinese soft-shelled turtle urinates through its mouth.

CREEPY CRAWLIES

Jurassic-era fleas were an inch long.

The Atlas moth of Southeast Asia is the largest moth in the world, with a total wing surface of sixty-five square inches and a ten-inch wingspan.

The Atlas moth does not have developed mouthparts and never eats during its one- to two-week adult lifespan, living on stored fats from the larval (caterpillar) stage.

When a caterpillar enters into its chrysalis, its body completely liquefies, and the butterfly is formed from scratch from its cells.

A virus that infects gypsy moth caterpillars causes them to climb to the top of trees, where they die and liquefy, raining down a virus-filled ooze on their brethren below.

Some ant species are incapable of foraging for food, tending their own young or their queen, or cleaning up their nests. Instead they raid the colonies of other ants and steal away their pupae, which they turn into slaves when the pupae reach adulthood.

The bite of the Brazilian wandering spider can cause painful, long-lasting erections in men, which can lead to impotence. The spider's venom is being studied for use in erectile dysfunction drugs.

Fire ants will latch on to one another to form large rafts when floodwaters strike. Some two hundred thousand ants may link together in a mat that can stay afloat for weeks. The ants on the bottom are able to breathe from air bubbles trapped between the mass of bodies.

While they suck blood, mosquitoes must urinate to prevent fluid overloads.

The male water boatman makes the loudest mating call, for its body size, of any animal. By rubbing their penis against ridges on their body, these 2.3-millimeter insects can make a noise that reaches ninety-nine decibels. Even when they are submerged in a river, their calls can be heard along its banks.

A new species of cockroach discovered in South Africa can jump a distance of fifty times its body length.

Centipedes are flatter than millipedes, with longer legs, and they move much quicker.

Millipedes generally have between 36 and 400 legs, although one California species has 750.

The oldest known land creature is a millipede species that lived some 428 million years ago.

There were eight-foot long millipedes roaming the Earth 300 million years ago. The largest species today measures over fifteen inches and lives in East Africa.

When threatened, millipedes will emit a hydrogen cyanide gas to ward off predators.

A termite queen can live for twenty-five to fifty years.

Termite colonies also contain kings, who mate with the queens for life.

Male Australian jewel beetles can't seem to differentiate between the dimpled, brown bottom of a beer bottle and the females of their species. The amorous males will try to mate with bottles and often die of overexertion after not being able to successfully complete the union.

JAWS

Anacondas have reverse curved teeth, and once they bite into a victim they cannot let go. They must relax their jaw for about thirty minutes to do so.

Alligator and crocodile jaws are covered with an array of tiny sensors that make them more sensitive than a human fingertip.

TONGUE TWISTERS

Anteaters belong to the taxonomic suborder *Vermilingua*, which means "worm tongue."

An anteater's tongue is coated with a sticky saliva that makes catching ants and termites easier.

To avoid wiping out a colony, and with it their source of food, an anteater will only feed a few minutes at a time at each colony.

Anteaters will occasionally dine on fruit and bird's eggs.

Anteaters have no teeth and digest their food whole with the aid of dirt and pebbles ingested while feeding.

TERMINEX

A numbat is a small marsupial also known as a banded anteater, found only in Western Australia, that feeds almost exclusively on termites. Adult numbats must eat at least 20,000 termites a day.

> Numbats are the only marsupial that is fully active by day.

Female marsupials have three vaginas. Two receive sperm from the male and the third delivers the young.

> Kangaroos cannot walk. They only can jump. They cannot jump backwards.

A LITTLE GREEN

The world's smallest vertebrate—a frog measuring just 7.7mm—was discovered in Papua New Guinea. The little guy can fit on the face of a dime, with plenty of room to spare. Unlike other frogs, which go through a tadpole stage before becoming adults, these guys skip this stage and are born as adults.

TOP DOGS

Dogs were first domesticated in numerous places independently, as early as thirty-three thousand years ago.

Today there are 185 different dog breeds in the Westminster Kennel Club Show. Six new breeds were admitted in 2012. They are:

- The American English coonhound, which was evolved from Virginia hounds that were descended from English foxhounds

- The Cesky terrier, which is a hunting dog that originated in the Czech Republic in 1950

- The Entlebucher mountain dog, which is native to Switzerland

- The Finnish lapphund, which is a reindeer herder

- The Norwegian lundehund, also known as the "puffin dog," which has six toes on each foot for scaling rocky coastal cliffs to hunt for puffins (though puffin hunting is now illegal)

- The Xoloitzcuintli, or "show low," formerly known as the Mexican hairless, which is the national dog of Mexico

The top eight most expensive dog breeds are:

- Pembroke Welsh corgi: $1,000

- Saluki: $2,500

- Chow Chow: between $1,000 and $8,500

- Egyptian pharaoh hound: between $2,500 and $6,500

- Löwchen: between $5,000 and $8,000

- Canadian Eskimo dog: $7,000

- Old English bulldog: $9,000

- Tibetan mastiff: between $2,000 and $7,000. Big Splash, or "Hong Dong," is an exceptional red Tibetan mastiff that sold for $1.6 million to a Chinese coal baron in 2012, a world record price for any dog. The breed, which weighs 180 pounds, is highly priced because these dogs are considered to be pure "Chinese" and rarely found outside Tibet. Genghis Khan and Buddha are believed to have kept them. Matings with this dog go for about $100,000 a pop.

BY A NOSE

The nose of a dog has a flap in the nostrils that deflects exhaled air to the sides, which prevents incoming scents from being blown away.

Dogs can get a sunburn on their nose.

BEWARE OF DOG

U.S. Navy Seal dogs wear protective vests that cost $20,000 and sport video cameras, microphones, and speakers, so that the dog's handlers can give it commands remotely—even to kill.

Approximately 92 percent of fatal dog attacks involve male dogs, and 94 percent of those dogs were not neutered.

Dog bites accounted for one-third of all homeowner insurance policy claims paid out in 2011.

PAMPERED PETS

In the United States, 53 percent of dogs and 55 percent of cats are overweight; 21 percent of dogs and 25 percent of cats are obese. These weight issues shorten the animals' lives by an average of 2.5 years.

UPON FURTHER REVIEW

Bulls cannot see the color red.

Lemmings do not intentionally commit mass suicide by jumping off cliffs. They have, however, been seen to run over the edge of a precipice in unfamiliar territory. The suicide myth was promoted by the 1958 Disney nature documentary *White Wilderness*, where lemmings were pushed into a river by a rotating platform installed by the film crew.

ESCAPE ARTISTS

Rabbits go into a trance when placed on their back. This is a survival instinct to fool a predator into thinking they are dead, allowing them to escape.

The African spiny mouse has the unique ability to shed large amounts of its skin to escape a predator. Even more amazing is the fact that it can then regrow the lost skin perfectly with no scarring, which no other mammal can do.

The African crested rat chews on poison tree bark and then spits the saliva onto its fur, where special porous hairs absorb the poison spit. This protects the little guys from being eaten by predators.

STEWED SHREWS

The Malaysian pen-tailed shrew nightly drinks the equivalent of nine glasses of wine in the form of a naturally occurring fermented nectar.

BY A WHISKER

The whiskers on a harbor seal are known as "vibrissae."

Moose with antlers have much improved hearing. The antlers act like a giant hearing aid, functioning like a parabolic reflector to collect and direct sound waves to the moose's ears.

Along with giant pandas, most species of mole have six digits per leg.

The male platypus produces a venom cocktail in its ankle spurs that has eighty types of toxins that can incapacitate a human.

Wombat poop is cube-shaped.

STAR POWER

PACKIN' HEAT

The following celebrities are gun owners: Angelina Jolie, Brad Pitt, Howard Stern, Joe Perry, Donald Trump, Eric Clapton, Christian Slater, James Earl Jones, and, of course, Clint Eastwood.

NAME THAT STAR

Stevie Wonder's given name is Stevland Hardaway Morris.

Wolfgang Puck's real name is Wolfgang Johannes Topfschnig.

Shakira's real name is Isabel Mebarak Ripoll.

Mel Brooks was born Melvin Kaminsky.

Reese Witherspoon named her son Tennessee.

Robert Downey Jr. named his son Exton Elias.

Man vs. Wild star Bear Grylls has sons named Marmaduke and Huckleberry.

Uma Thurman's daughter is named Rosalind Arusha Arkadina Altalune Florence Thurman-Busson.

Mariah Carey named her two children with Nick Cannon Monroe and Morocco (because Cannon proposed to her in a Moroccan-style room in her mansion). She calls the kids Roc and Roe.

Beyoncé and Jay-Z tried to trademark their baby's first name—Blue Ivy—but were rebuffed by the court.

SOUNDS FAMILIAR

Mila Kunis is the voice of Meg Griffin on *Family Guy*.

Casey Kasem was the voice of Shaggy on *Scooby-Doo*.

Fergie was the voice of Charlie Brown's little sister Sally on a couple of *Peanuts* specials.

Seth Green voiced Chris Griffin on *Family Guy*.

Jerry Orbach, who starred on *Law & Order*, was the voice of Lumiere in Disney's *Beauty and the Beast*.

HAPPILY NEVER AFTER

Singer Sinead O'Connor married her fourth husband, Barry Herridge, from the back of a pink Cadillac in Las Vegas. The honeymoon didn't last long. They were divorced sixteen days later.

Nicolas Cage was married to Lisa Marie Presley for 108 days.

Kenny Chesney and Renée Zellweger made it for 130 days.

Drew Barrymore was married to bartender Jeremy Thomas for fewer than two months and filed divorce papers after five months of marriage to comedian Tom Green.

Britney Spears's marriage to Jason Alexander lasted fifty-five hours.

The only one of Elizabeth Taylor's seven husbands she did not divorce was producer Michael Todd, who died in 1958, a year after they were married. Todd perished when his private plane, the *Lucky Liz*, crashed in New Mexico. The plane was overloaded, flying too high for its design, and had icy wings. Taylor had wanted to accompany him on the flight, but he made her stay home because she had a cold.

WHAT HAPPENS IN VEGAS . . .

Not everything that happens in Vegas stays in Vegas. Janeane Garofalo discovered in 2012 that she had been married for some twenty years to writer/producer Rob Cohen. The two went to a Las Vegas drive-thru wedding chapel in a taxi in 1992. Apparently she didn't think weddings in Vegas were legally binding.

BRING THE BLING

Movie producer Michael Todd gave Elizabeth Taylor a thirty-carat diamond engagement ring in 1957.

Jay-Z gave Beyoncé an eighteen-carat diamond when he popped the question in 2008.

Mariah Carey accepted a seventeen-carat pink diamond from Nick Cannon in 2008 after dating for six weeks.

Donald Trump gave Melania Knauss a twelve-carat rock in 2004.

Grace Kelly got a ten-and-a-half-carat ring from Monaco's Prince Rainier III in 1955.

HERE'S JOHNNY!

Johnny Carson's television career began in Omaha, Nebraska, in 1950. He hosted a local show called *The Squirrel's Nest*, where one of his bits was interviewing pigeons on top of the courthouse about the political corruption they had seen.

Carson's big break came in 1954, when, as a writer for the popular *Red Skelton Show*, he was asked to fill in at the last minute after Skelton had accidentally been knocked out just before airtime.

Johnny at first turned down hosting *The Tonight Show*, but after Joey Bishop, Jackie Gleason, Groucho Marx, and Bob Newhart also declined, NBC convinced him to accept.

HOLLYWOOD CONFIDENTIAL

Director Tim Burton once played water polo and was on his high school swim team.

Sarah Jessica Parker's tenth great-grandmother was accused of being a witch in the Salem witchcraft trials.

Director James Cameron was once a school bus driver, as was John Malkovich.

Cuba Gooding Jr. was a backup dancer for Lionel Richie.

Brad Pitt had his front teeth chipped for his role in *Fight Club*, then had them redone afterward.

Mick Jagger studied at the London School of Economics and had planned on being an accountant.

Ken Jeong of *The Hangover* is a medical doctor who studied at the University of North Carolina. He broke into comedy by doing stand-up in his spare time.

Colin Farrell has a lucky belt and always wears the same boxer shorts, with shamrocks, on the first day of shooting a new movie.

Heidi Klum carries a bag of her baby teeth for good luck.

Reese Witherspoon's father is a bigamist.

In 1935, unmarried actress Loretta Young conceived a child with Clark Gable while filming *The Call of the Wild*. Young had the baby in secret and put her into orphanages until she turned nineteen months, at which time she brought the child home and told the public that she had adopted her. In 1940, when Young married Thomas Lewis, the girl, Judy, took his surname. Until her dying day, Young never publicly acknowledged Judy as her biological daughter.

Comedian Jimmie "J.J." Walker, of *Good Times* fame, once employed both Jay Leno and David Letterman as writers for $150 a week.

After the cancellation of *Star Trek* and a divorce from his wife, William Shatner lived in his car for a time.

Lucille Ball filed for divorce from Desi Arnaz the day after they filmed the last episode of *I Love Lucy*.

Johnny Depp appeared as a guy named Eddie in a 1991 music video for Tom Petty's song "Into the Great Wide Open."

Christina Aguilera made a Spanish language album—*Mi Reflejo*—in 2000, even though she doesn't speak the language.

Richard Gere played the part of Danny Zuko in the stage production of *Grease* in 1973, five years before John Travolta rose to fame playing the role in the 1978 movie adaptation.

Kelly Bensimon of *The Real Housewives of New York City* is not a housewife, or any other kind of wife. She was divorced in 2007.

Richard Belzer holds the record for playing the same character in the most different TV series. He has appeared as Detective John Munch on at least eleven different shows, including *Homicide, Homicide: Life on the Street, Law & Order: Trial by Jury, Law & Order: SVU, The X-Files, The Beat, M.O.N.Y., Sesame Street, The Wire, Arrested Development,* and *30 Rock.*

Daniel Radcliffe admits to showing up on the set drunk from the night before while filming the later Harry Potter movies.

Pat Sajak confided that he and Vanna White would down up to six margaritas during their breaks between the shooting of several *Wheel of Fortune* shows per day.

LeAnn Rimes has a tattoo on her right foot that reads, "the only one that matters." It's something husband Eddie Cibrian said to her.

Michael Richards was slated to play the title character on *Monk* on ABC. He backed out and then so did ABC. The show was then picked up by USA Network, starring Tony Shalhoub.

Kate Upton's great grandfather was a cofounder of Whirlpool.

David Bowie's left eye is permanently dilated from being punched in the face as a kid.

Gossip Girl star Leighton Meester was born in prison, where her mother was doing time for being involved in a drug ring.

Frank Oz is the puppeteer who performed Yoda, Miss Piggy, and the Cookie Monster, among others.

Katie Couric battled bulimia in college.

Pierce Brosnan used to work as a fire-eater in a circus.

During one week in November 1994, Tim Allen had the top movie (*The Santa Clause*), the top TV show (*Home Improvement*), and the top *New York Times* best-selling book (*Don't Stand Too Close to a Naked Man*).

Jane Lynch met director Christopher Guest while shooting a Frosted Flakes commercial. The two went on to work together on several "mockumentary" movie projects, including *Best in Show* and *A Mighty Wind*.

CULT OF PERSONALITIES

Notable celebrity Scientologists include Kirstie Alley, Anne Archer, Karen Black, Sonny Bono, Jeff Conaway, Chick Corea, Tom Cruise, Isaac Hayes, Juliette Lewis, Priscilla Presley, Kelly Preston, Leah Remini, John Travolta, Greta Van Susteren, and Edgar Winter.

People who were once Scientologists include Al Jarreau, Charles Manson, and Lisa Marie Presley.

SELLEBRITIES

Rihanna once promoted Secret (deodorant) Body Spray.

Serena Williams hawked Tampax.

Ozzy Osbourne shilled for "I Can't Believe It's Not Butter."

Florence Henderson pushed Polident.

Kris Jenner promoted Poise pads.

Justin Bieber has his own line of Opi nail polish.

50 Cent has planned to start his own line of condoms.

WHAT PRICE BEAUTY?

Jennifer Aniston spends about four hundred dollars a day on beauty. She uses a $450 neck ointment, a $350 rejuvenating serum, gets $295 laser skin peels and $450 facials, $600 hair cuts, $320 highlights, and spends $900 a week on yoga sessions.

JUST A CLICK AWAY

Justin Bieber was the most-searched-for celebrity on the Bing search engine top ten list for 2011. The next nine were Kim Kardashian, Jennifer Aniston, Lindsay Lohan, Megan Fox, Jennifer Lopez, Britney Spears, Katy Perry, Lady Gaga, and Miley Cyrus.

Yahoo! reported that the top-searched athletes for 2011 were Danica Patrick (race car driver), Tiger Woods, Manny Pacquiao (boxer), Maria Sharapova (tennis player), Serena Williams, Kris Humphries (basketball player briefly married to Kim Kardashian), Hope Solo (soccer player), Kobe Bryant, Lamar Odom (basketball player), and Caroline Wozniacki (tennis player).

Lady Gaga had the most Twitter followers in 2011, with 14.4 million. Kim Kardashian had 10.3 million and Britney Spears had 10 million.

One can now download an app to have Snoop Dogg as the voice on a TomTom GPS device.

BACKWORDS

Several well-known celebs have suffered from dyslexia, including Jewel, Bruce Jenner, Kurt Cobain, Orlando Bloom, Whoopi Goldberg, Cher, Patrick Dempsey, Vince Vaughn, Keanu Reeves, Keira Knightley, and Tony Bennett.

WHAT MIGHT HAVE BEEN

Christopher Walken, Al Pacino, and Nick Nolte were all considered for the role of Han Solo in *Star Wars,* instead of Harrison Ford.

Al Pacino was considered, along with Christopher Reeve, for the lead in *Pretty Woman*, instead of Richard Gere.

Molly Ringwald, Heather Locklear, Kim Basinger, and Meg Ryan were all thought of before Julia Roberts for *Pretty Woman.*

Nicolas Cage was in the running with Mickey Rourke for the lead in *The Wrestler.*

Gwyneth Paltrow almost beat out Kate Winslet for the part of Rose in *Titanic*.

Val Kilmer could have been the one hitting the floor with Jennifer Grey in *Dirty Dancing*, instead of Patrick Swayze.

Kate Winslet nearly beat out Renée Zellweger for the lead in *Bridget Jones's Diary*.

Tom Cruise was the first choice to play Henry Hill in *Goodfellas*, not Ray Liotta.

RACIST ROLES

Many older movies chose to cast white actors as characters of another race, usually with embarrassing results:

Charlton Heston was cast as a Mexican drug agent in 1958's *Touch of Evil*. His skin and hair were darkened and he wore a cheesy mustache.

John Wayne played Genghis Khan in the 1956 film *The Conqueror*. His eyes were taped back at the corners and he sported a bad glue-on goatee.

Mickey Rooney portrayed a Japanese character in *Breakfast at Tiffany's*. His buckteeth, near-sighted glasses, and horrible accent would be considered offensive today.

Keanu Reeves played Buddha in 1993's *Little Buddha*.

TAXING TIMES

Chris Tucker owes the Internal Revenue Service millions of dollars and has had his $6 million home foreclosed on.

Joe Francis, the *Girls Gone Wild* guy, went to jail for owing $34 million in back taxes.

In 1996, Burt Reynolds filed for bankruptcy and was $10 million in debt.

In 1998 and 2010, Toni Braxton filed for bankruptcy and had to take court-ordered financial classes.

BAD ACTS

Actor Jamie Waylett, who played the villain Crabbe in the *Harry Potter* movie series, was arrested for looting and possession of a homemade bomb, during the 2011 riots in London.

Joe Son, the martial arts expert/actor who played the character Random Task, Dr. Evil's henchman in the movie *Austin Powers: International Man of Mystery*, is serving a life sentence for the rape and torture of a girl in 1990. In 2011, he killed his cellmate and was moved to solitary confinement.

Cameron Douglas, the son of Oscar-winner Michael Douglas, was sent to prison for dealing drugs in 2010. Four and a half years were added to his sentence in 2011, after he was found with drugs in jail.

In 1978, Tim Allen was arrested for drug trafficking after he was found to have 650 grams of cocaine. Allen served just over two years in prison.

CRADLE ROBBERS

In 2012, eighty-six-year-old Dick Van Dyke married his forty-year-old makeup artist.

Eighty-six-year-old Hugh Hefner topped that, marrying twenty-six-year-old Playmate Crystal Harris in 2012.

Fifty-year-old Doug Hutchison, who starred in *The Green Mile*, married Courtney Stodden when she was just sixteen.

Forty-nine-year-old Linda Hogan, former wife of Hulk Hogan, dated one of her kids' high school classmates after the split with Hulk—nineteen-year-old Charley Hill.

In 1993, thirty-eight-year-old Jerry Seinfeld began dating high school senior Shoshanna Lonstein, who was seventeen at the time.

Twenty-nine-year-old Milo Ventimiglia dated *Heroes* co-star Hayden Panettiere when she was seventeen.

MAN ABOUT TOWN

Singer John Mayer is quite the ladies' man. He has dated Katy Perry, Taylor Swift, Jennifer Aniston, Minka Kelly, Jessica Simpson, and Jennifer Love Hewitt.

Mayer wrote the song "Your Body Is a Wonderland" about Hewitt. She is quoted as having said, "My body is more like a pawn shop."

SCARRED FOR LIFE

Tina Fey has a scar on the left side of her face from a nasty cut she received when she was five years old.

Marilyn Monroe had a big scar on her stomach, which is the reason there are very few photographs of her midsection.

Elizabeth Taylor underwent a tracheotomy in 1960 that left a scar at the base of her throat.

Catherine Zeta-Jones, likewise, has a visible tracheotomy scar obtained in childhood.

Sharon Stone has a rope burn scar on her neck from the time she rode a horse into a clothesline.

Joaquin Phoenix has a cleft lip.

Victoria's Secret supermodel Karolína Kurková has an extraordinarily smooth belly button due to a procedure that she had as an infant.

Mary J. Blige has a scar under her left eye, and Sandra Bullock has one over her left eye.

Queen Latifah has a scar on the top of her forehead.

GOOD FENCES MAKE GROUCHY NEIGHBORS

Ozzy and Sharon Osbourne were sued in 2012 for building a fence to encompass roughly 8,500 square feet of a neighboring property's land.

THE MOUTH THAT ROARED

Rush Limbaugh has the largest listening audience on talk radio, followed by Sean Hannity and Michael Savage.

RISKY BUSINESS

Eighty percent of Hollywood movies are insured by Fireman's Fund Insurance during production, covering the actors, props, wardrobes, and equipment.

Insurance accounts for about 1 to 3 percent of a film's budget.

The more dangerous stunts involved in a movie, the more it costs to insure. The riskiest movies to insure in recent years, according to Fireman's, were *The Girl with the Dragon Tattoo*, because of the motorcycle chases and torture scenes; *Salt*, where Angelina Jolie did her own stunts; *Inglorious Basterds*; *2012*; *Crazy Heart*; *Nine*; *The Wrestler*; and *Into the Wild*, where props had to be flown to Alaska and bears were used.

JUST IN CASE

Over the years, celebrities have taken out insurance policies on various body parts. Singer Tom Jones once insured his chest hair for $7 million. Jennifer Lopez insured her butt for $27 million. Pittsburgh Steeler Troy Polamalu insured his long dark hair for $1 million. David Lee Roth got a policy in case one of his sperm accidentally impregnated one of his many partners. Heidi Klum insured her legs for $2.2 million, and Mariah Carey insured her gams for a whopping $1 billion! *Ugly Betty* star America Ferrera insured her smile for $10 million. Dolly Parton's assets were insured for $300,000 per boob. David Beckham insured against a career-ending injury for $151 million. Rod Stewart insured his raspy voice for $7 million. Keith Richards insured his middle finger for $1.6 million, lest he not be able to flip people off anymore.

MOVIE MAGIC

The distance shots in the tornado scene in *The Wizard of Oz* were of a real twister. The mid-range shots were created by coiling a stocking. The close-up images used a burlap bag full of dust.

The nasty boy next door in *Toy Story* had exactly 15,977 computer-generated hairs on his head. The trees had up to ten thousand leaves each.

In *Star Wars, Episode I: The Phantom Menace*, the communicator Qui-Gon Jinn uses is a modified Gillette for Women Sensor Excel razor.

HOME ON LOAN

The suburban Chicago Georgian-style mansion used in the filming of *Home Alone* sold in 2012 for $1.585 million. The family that owned it lived in the house during the six-month shooting of the blockbuster movie. The owner's daughter became playmates with the eight-year-old star of the flick, Macaulay Culkin.

HOT MOVIES

Early movies were shot on nitrate film base, which is extremely flammable. There were many movie house fires as a result of film igniting in the projector.

In the 1920s, Hollywood made twice as many films a year as it does today.

MISOGYNIST MOVIES

Two-thirds of speaking roles in movies go to men.

Eighty percent of Hollywood producers, directors, and writers are men.

RATINGS GAME

The Motion Picture Association of America (MPAA) movie rating system is followed voluntarily by theater operators. There are no local, state, or federal laws governing who can see what films. The ratings are just a suggestion.

From 1970 to 1972, there were four movie ratings—G, GP, R, and X. Then from 1972 to 1984 they were—G, PG, R, and X. In 1984, there was an uproar over the PG rating of Steven Spielberg's two rather violent films *Gremlins* and *Indiana Jones and the Temple of Doom*. Spielberg encouraged the MPAA to add a fifth rating—PG-13—for movies too intense for PG but not deserving of an R rating.

The first movie to be released with a PG-13 rating was *Red Dawn*, in 1984.

In 1990, the X rating was replaced by the NC-17 rating. *Henry & June* was the first film to get this rating.

Midnight Cowboy was rated X when it was released in 1969. When it was re-released, unedited, in 1971, it was rated R.

The MPAA has no written rules for how to rate a movie, and ratings can seem inconsistent. Most films can use the word "fuck" up to four times in a non-sexual context and still get a PG-13 rating. The word "pussy" was even allowed in the PG-13 films *Super 8* and *Transformers: Revenge of the Fallen*.

PIRATE COVE

The motion picture industry sued Sony Betamax (an early video recording format) to prevent the use of their system for home recording purposes. The U.S. Supreme Court ruled in 1984 that it is not copyright infringement to record television shows at home for personal use.

Avatar is the most pirated movie of all time, with 21 million illegal downloads as of 2011. *The Dark Knight* and *Transformers* tie for second place, with 19 million downloads each.

Game of Thrones was the most illegally downloaded TV show in 2012.

WRETCHED RATCHED

Actress Louise Fletcher, who won an Oscar for her portrayal of Nurse Ratched in *One Flew Over the Cuckoo's Nest*, now finds her performance of the wicked RN so disturbing that she can no longer watch the movie.

BACK TO THE FRIDGE

In the first draft of the script for *Back to the Future*, the time machine was a refrigerator. Steven Spielberg changed his mind because he didn't want children climbing into refrigerators, plus the DeLorean was much cooler looking.

ALTERNATE REALITY

The Discovery Channel "reality" show *Moonshiners* was eventually revealed to be a scam. The supposed moonshiners trying to evade the Virginia authorities were not really distilling spirits in their stills. The producers duped Virginia authorities into believing they were making a documentary and thus gained their cooperation with the series.

Storage Wars performer David Hester revealed that the producers of the show often plant interesting and valuable items for the cast to find. He also maintains the bidding that takes place on the series is rigged.

POTTER'S PLACE

In *Harry Potter and the Chamber of Secrets*, a picture of Gandalf the Grey, from *The Lord of the Rings*, can be seen hanging on Dumbledore's wall of wizards.

Actress Shirley Henderson, who was in her late thirties at the time, played fourteen-year-old Moaning Myrtle in *Harry Potter and the Chamber of Secrets* and *Harry Potter and the Goblet of Fire*.

The name Voldemort derives from the French, meaning "flight from death," which is what Voldemort does in the books.

During the filming of *Chamber of Secrets* there was an infestation of lice among the child actors.

The *Harry Potter* series were the first children's books to make the *New York Times* Bestseller List since *Charlotte's Web* in 1952.

The final installment of the *Harry Potter* book series—*Harry Potter and the Deathly Hallows*—sold 11 million copies in just twenty-four hours.

PROLIFIC PERFORMERS

Actor John Carradine holds the record for appearing in the most films, more than three hundred. The total is higher if movies he appeared uncredited in are counted.

John Wayne was the most commercially successful actor of all time and *starred* in the most movies—142.

BEAUTY *AND* BRAINS

The beautiful Austrian-American film star Hedy Lamarr was also a mathematical genius. During World War II, she came up with an early technique for frequency hopping and spread-spectrum communications that is still used today for Wi-Fi, Bluetooth, and wireless phones.

Lamarr also holds the distinction of performing the first female orgasm on screen, in the 1933 movie *Ecstasy*, and was the first to show full female frontal nudity.

MOVIE BUFFS

Artist's model Audrey Munson was the first woman to appear nude in a film. She played an artist's model in 1915's *Inspiration*.

The 1916 silent film *A Daughter of the Gods*, starring Australian swimming star Annette Kellerman, was the first movie where a major star appeared nude.

REBELS REQUIEM

The three stars of *Rebel Without a Cause* all met tragic ends in real life. James Dean died in a car wreck. Natalie Wood drowned under suspicious circumstances. Sal Mineo was stabbed in a parking area behind his West Hollywood home.

BUILDING BRIDGES

In the movie *The Bridge on the River Kwai*, the prisoners built the bridge in two months. The construction company hired to build the bridge for the film took eight months to complete the task.

In real life, some eighty thousand Asian conscripts and thirteen thousand prisoners died during the building of the bridge for the Japanese in 1943. Two bridges were built, a temporary wooden one and a permanent steel-and-concrete one.

The bridges were destroyed by Allied bombers two years later. The steel bridge has since been repaired and is still in use today.

A real bridge and train were destroyed for the movie. On the first take, the explosive charges failed to detonate and the train went over the bridge and crashed down a hill.

OUTTAKES

At least thirty-two different actresses were screen-tested for the role of Scarlett O'Hara in *Gone with the Wind*, even Lucille Ball.

In *Terminator 2*, Arnold Schwarzenegger was paid $15 million and only had seven hundred words of dialogue. That comes out to $21,429 per word.

The blue pinafore dress Judy Garland wore as Dorothy in *The Wizard of Oz* sold for $480,000 in 2012.

A "cold open" is when a TV show or movie jumps directly into the plot, before the opening credits roll.

TV shows do this to hook the viewer before going to the first commercial break.

For the scene in the Alfred Hitchcock movie *The Birds* where Tippi Hedren is attacked, trained birds were attached to her with nylon strings. Hedren actually was cut by a bird during the filming.

During the filming of the 1931 movie *Viking*, a ship explosion killed the producer and about twenty-six members of the crew while they were filming an iceberg off of Labrador.

The 1964 movie *The Fall of the Roman Empire* had the biggest outdoor movie set ever built. Its reconstruction of the Roman Forum measured 1,312 feet by 754 feet.

In the movie *Transformers: Dark of the Moon*, 532 cars were destroyed. They were flood-damaged autos donated by an insurance company.

TO BOLDLY GO . . .

Initially, NBC executives wanted to ditch the Spock character from *Star Trek* because they thought he looked satanic.

James Doohan, who played Scottie on *Star Trek*, lost his right middle finger during World War II.

Lieutenant Uhura's name means "freedom" in Swahili.

Star Trek: The Next Generation character Geordi La Forge was named for an avid *Star Trek* fan, George La Forge, who died of muscular dystrophy in 1975.

Captain Kirk's USS *Enterprise* NCC-1701 is 953.7 feet long.

It would take the starship *Enterprise* 400,000 years to cross the galaxy on impulse drive.

The *Enterprise* holds a crew of 430.

Klingons like to eat food that is still alive.

A Vulcan's heart beats several hundred times a minute, and Vulcans don't have an appendix.

BONDAGE

The only James Bond movie theme song to hit number one on the *Billboard* Hot 100 chart was "A View to a Kill," by Duran Duran. "Live and Let Die," by Paul McCartney and Wings, and "Nobody Does it Better," by Carly Simon, made it to number two. "For Your Eyes Only," by Sheena Easton, hit number five, and "Die Another Day," by Madonna, and "Skyfall," by Adele, both peaked at number eight.

"OH TAY!"

Alfalfa of *Our Gang* film shorts (later known as *The Little Rascals*, when they moved to television) fame was actor Carl Switzer.

Switzer was shot to death by an acquaintance in a dispute over money in 1959.

George McFarland, who played Spanky, got his nickname from a newspaper reporter who called the three-year-old actor a "spanky child," a term at the time referring to a bright toddler.

McFarland, who was in the series from 1932 to 1942, popularized the expression "okeydokey."

William "Billie" Thomas Jr. played Buckwheat in the series from 1934 to 1944. Originally, Buckwheat was a girl, but later she slowly morphed into a boy.

Thomas suffered from a speech impediment and is best known for the expression "O-tay!"

Thomas's family were offended by Eddie Murphy's spoof of the Buckwheat character on *Saturday Night Live* in the 1980s.

In 1990, the ABC newsmagazine TV show *20/20* did an interview with an Arizona grocery bagger that they thought was Thomas. Unfortunately, Thomas had died ten years earlier. ABC apologized and the program's producer was forced to resign.

Contrary to popular myth, Bill Cosby never bought up the rights to *Our Gang* to keep the show's racial stereotypes off TV.

A pit bull, with a black ring around its left eye, played Petey. The ring was applied by makeup artist Max Factor.

Mickey Rooney and Shirley Temple both auditioned for *Our Gang*.

OFF TO A GOOD START

In 2010, *TV Guide* published a list of the top ten television credits sequences. They were, in order, *The Simpsons*, *Get Smart*, *The Mary Tyler Moore Show*, *Hawaii Five-O* (the original), *True Blood*, *The Big Bang Theory*, *Dexter*, *The Brady Bunch*, *Mad Men*, and *The Sopranos*.

BEWARE THE BLOB

In 1950, four Philadelphia policemen saw a six-foot, round, light-emitting, gelatinous mass land on the ground and begin to climb up a telephone pole. This incident became the basis for the 1958 cult classic *The Blob*, which was filmed in the suburbs of Philadelphia.

The Blob was Steve McQueen's first starring role.

The movie's title song—"The Blob"—hit number thirty-three on the *Billboard* Hot 100 list.

BLINDED BY THE LIGHT

CNN news personality Anderson Cooper sunburned his eyes in 2012, after spending several hours on the water in Portugal without sunglasses. He was blind for thirty-six hours.

SOAP DOPE

It costs about $50 million a year to produce a daytime soap opera, about 30 percent more than it costs to produce a television talk show.

In 1999, there were eleven American soap operas on television. In 2011, there were only four.

MUSICAL MOMENTS

The only three songs to hit number one on the *Billboard* Hot 100 chart after the death of the recording artist were "(Sittin' on) The Dock of the Bay" by Otis Redding, "Time in a Bottle" by Jim Croce, and "Me and Bobby McGee" by Janice Joplin.

According to *Billboard*, Adele's *21* was the bestselling album of 2011 and 2012, selling 5.82 million copies and 4.41 million copies, respectively.

The bikini didn't really catch on until the number one hit song "Itsy Bitsy Teenie Weenie Yellow Polka Dot Bikini" was released in 1960, by sixteen-year-old Brian Hyland.

South Korean rap star Psy's music video "Gangnam Style" is the most-watched item posted to YouTube, with more than 1.5 billion views.

A poll by UltimateClassicRock.com found that the top country rock song of all time is "Can't You See" by the Marshall Tucker Band. The rest of the top ten in order are "Sweet Home Alabama" by Lynyrd Skynyrd, "Green Grass and High Tides" by the Outlaws, "Highway Song" by Blackfoot, "Long Haired Country Boy" by the Charlie Daniels Band, "Flirtin' with Disaster" by Molly Hatchet, "La Grange" by ZZ Top, "Ramblin' Man" by the Allman Brothers, "30 Days in the Hole" by Humble Pie, and "Mississippi Queen" by Mountain.

The top-earning musicians for 2012 were Dr. Dre at $110 million, Roger Waters at $88 million, Elton John at $80 million, U2 at $78 million, Take That at $69 million, Bon Jovi at $60 million, Britney Spears at $58 million, Paul McCartney at $57 million, Taylor Swift at $57 million, Justin Bieber at $55 million, and Toby Keith at $55 million.

Trumpeter Louis Armstrong used to get hard calluses on his lips, which he would remove himself every four or five years with a razor blade.

Johann Sebastian Bach wrote some 1,100 pieces of music.

Wolfgang Amadeus Mozart started playing the harpsichord at the age of three and composing music at the age of five.

Mozart began a three-and-a-half-year musical tour of Europe with his family when he was only six.

Mozart went on to compose enough music to fill two hundred compact discs.

BOOK CLUB

Toni Morrison is the pen name of Chloe Anthony Wofford.

George Orwell was the nom de plume of Eric Arthur Blair.

Anne Rice was named after her father—Howard Allen O'Brien. She hated the name Howard and told the nuns on her first day of kindergarten that her name was Anne. Her last name comes from her husband Stan Rice.

Voltaire was born François-Marie Arouet.

Mystery writer Agatha Christie was the first known woman in Britain to take up surfing, in the 1920s.

Emily Dickinson was a recluse who didn't leave her house for more than twenty years and spoke to visitors through a closed door.

PAINTIN' PLACE

When Grant Wood was fourteen, he won third place in a national crayon drawing contest sponsored by Crayola. He credits this with sparking his interest in becoming an artist.

Michelangelo had his nose broken by a contemporary artist named Torrigiano, and was disfigured for life.

The Louvre was built in the late 1100s as a fortress.

Paul Gaugin worked as a laborer on the Panama Canal construction project. He was fired after two weeks.

In 2012, guitarist Eric Clapton sold the painting *Abstraktes Bild (809-4)* by German artist Gerhard Richter, for $34,190,756, a new record price for the work of a living painter. That's more then ten times what Clapton paid for it in 2001. The previous record was for the Jasper Johns work titled *Flags*, which sold for $28.6 million in 2010.

DEADLY DATA

The city of Chicago averages more than one murder a day.

Each day in America, 6,718 people die. That's one death every thirteen seconds. There is one birth every eight seconds.

The Centers for Disease Control and Prevention (CDC) reports that the number of Americans who die from prescription drug overdoses is greater than that for cocaine and heroin overdoses combined. In 2008, there were 20,044 overdose deaths from prescription drugs, 14,800 of those from painkillers.

The most common cause of poisonings in America is analgesics, at 12 percent, followed by cosmetics/personal care products, household cleaners, sedatives/antipsychotics/hypnotics, and foreign bodies/toys/miscellaneous.

NO COUNTRY FOR OLD MEN

For every one hundred women in the United States that is a centenarian (over one hundred years old), there are only 20.7 men.

In New Mexico, people over the age of one hundred who are not dependents pay no income tax.

INTIMATE INJURIES

Sixteen thousand American men and women seek treatment in emergency rooms every year for genital injuries.

IN THE LINE OF DUTY

In 2011, 163 American law enforcement officers were killed in the line of duty. Sixty-eight died from gunfire.

IN*DIE*PENDENCE DAY

According to a 2011 study, the deadliest day of the year on American highways is July 4, with 144 fatalities. The next five deadliest days are September 2, August 13, July 15, May 20, and November 11.

Fatal car wrecks increase by 6 percent on income tax filing day.

New Year's Day has the highest number of drunken driving–related deaths—130. It is also the day with the most pedestrians killed by vehicles, topping Halloween.

And the most dangerous day of the week to drive to work is . . . Friday.

The number of traffic and workplace accidents increase the day after daylight saving time begins. Heart attacks also increase by 20 percent.

One-half of those injured while wearing headphones are struck by trains.

CLICK IT OR TICKET

People in the West wear seat belts more than folks in other parts of America—94 percent. Those in the Northeast are least likely to buckle up—80 percent.

Drivers buckle up more on weekends and when in heavy traffic.

Seat belt usage reduces the risk of dying in a fatal accident by 45 percent for front seat occupants. It is estimated that seat belts saved 12,546 U.S. lives in 2010.

PILL POPPERS

People in the Eastern United States are more likely to use antibiotics than are those on the West Coast.

West Virginia had the highest rate of antibiotic use from 1999 to 2007—1,222 prescriptions per one thousand people, more than double the rate in Alaska—546 prescriptions per one thousand people—during the same time period.

The rate of antibiotic use in Scandinavia is much lower than Alaska's, as doctors there are trained not to prescribe the drugs for things they are useless against, such as viruses.

STAMP OUT HUNGER

Fifteen percent of the American population is on food stamps.

COLLEGE CONFIDENTIAL

In 2010, there were 723,277 foreign students enrolled in U.S. colleges. That's about 4 percent of overall American university enrollment.

China led the way with the highest number of students enrolled—158,000—followed by India, South Korea, Canada, Taiwan, Saudi Arabia, Japan, Vietnam, Mexico, and Turkey.

The University of Southern California led the nation in the number of foreign students enrolled in 2011, which it had done for the previous ten years.

In 2009, 19.2 percent of Hispanics in America had college degrees, as did 29.4 percent of blacks, 48.7 percent of whites, and 69.1 percent of Asians.

About 79 percent of American university faculty members are white.

Just 56 percent of American college students complete a four-year degree within six years. College dropouts tend to be male.

The publicly funded four-year colleges with the worst graduation rates are as follows: Southern University at New Orleans, Louisiana, graduates 4 percent; University of the District of Columbia, Washington, DC, 7.7 percent; Kent State University-East Liverpool, Ohio, 8.9 percent; Rogers State University, Claremore, Oklahoma, 11.5 percent; Texas Southern University, Houston, Texas, 13.3 percent; Ohio University Southern Campus, Ironton, Ohio, 13.7 percent; Kent State University-Tuscarawas, Ohio, 13.9 percent; Purdue University North Central, Indiana, 14 percent; Cameron University, Lawton, Oklahoma, 14.1 percent; and Ohio University at Chillicothe, Ohio, 15.6 percent.

The University of Pennsylvania was America's first nonreligious university.

About 96 percent of Ivy League professors who donated money in 2012 gave to Barack Obama in the presidential election.

LOCK AND LOAD

Colleges in five states permit students to carry guns on campus—Colorado, Mississippi, Oregon, Utah, and Wisconsin.

MAKE ROOM FOR THE TURKEY

November 15 is National Clean Out Your Refrigerator Day.

CHANGE FOR THE BETTER

There is a custom among Italian-Americans in the New York/North Jersey area to throw change on the floor of a new car for good luck.

PETITE PARKS

At just 0.02 acres in size, the smallest site in the National Park Service is the Thaddeus Kosciuszko National Memorial in Philadelphia, which honors the American Revolutionary War hero.

Another little known National Park Service site is the African Burial Ground in Manhattan. Here, the remains of seventeenth- and eighteenth-century slaves that were unearthed accidentally during a construction project in 1991 are commemorated with a monument and visitor center.

The Nicodemus National Historical Park in Nicodemus, Kansas, is the only remaining all-black town established west of the Mississippi. This town was used as an outpost for ex-slaves moving westward after the Civil War.

JOBS REPORT

Steve Jobs dropped out of school after one semester at Reed College in Oregon. He later went back to audit a course in calligraphy, which he credited with the simple design and elegance of Apple products.

After leaving college, Jobs backpacked across India while eating psychedelic mushrooms. He said this experience helped crystallize his vision and creativity.

He was fired by the Apple board of directors in 1985 for being too much of a perfectionist and a control freak. The company faltered during his absence and they rehired him in 1997.

Steve Jobs occasionally manned Apple's customer service phones and was known to have personally called a customer who had emailed him with a complaint about getting his laptop repaired.

Jobs would lease a different silver Mercedes SL55 AMG every six months. Because anyone with a new car in California has six months to affix a license plate, his cars never had one.

Per square foot of floor space, the most profitable stores in the world are Apple Retail Stores. They generate twice the income, per square foot, of Tiffany's.

A LITTLE FACE TIME

Just as fellow tech guru Steve Jobs did, Facebook founder Mark Zuckerberg wears the same thing every day. The billionaire claims to have one drawer with twenty identical gray T-shirts that make up his shirt wardrobe.

Zuckerberg announced that he only eats meat from animals that he has personally killed. The dead animals, which include goats, pigs, and chickens, are sent out for butchering.

When the share price of Facebook stock tumbled after being issued in 2012, Zuckerberg lost $8.1 billion in net worth by the end of the year.

'TIS BETTER TO GIVE . . .

The Americans who gave the most money to charity in 2011 were deceased agribusiness heiress Margaret Cargill, whose estate of $6 billion was left to a charitable trust; steel executive William Dietrich II, who gave away $500 million; Microsoft cofounder Paul Allen, who donated $373 million; financier George Soros, who doled out $335 million; and New York City mayor Michael Bloomberg, who gave away $311 million.

In 2012, Mark Zuckerberg gave $500 million in Facebook stock to a charitable foundation.

LUAU LARRY

Oracle CEO and billionaire Larry Ellison bought the sixth-largest Hawaiian Island in 2012. He now owns 98 percent of Lanai, and the state owns the other 2 percent.

DEER ME!

There were 13.7 million American hunters in 2011.

The majority of American deer hunters who get injured in the field do so by falling out of their tree stands.

MILITARY MATTERS

There were 167,000 women in the U.S. armed forces in 2010.

The U.S. military spent $700 billion on defense in 2011. That's more than the next seventeen highest-defense-spending countries combined.

The last living American veteran of World War I, Frank Buckles, died in 2011 at the age of 110.

Albert Woolson, the oldest living veteran of the Civil War, died in 1956 at the age of 109.

The oldest documented veteran of the American Revolution was one Lemuel Cook, who died in 1866 at age 106.

In 2010, there were 144,842 homeless veterans in the United States.

One in 150 veterans is homeless.

Apporximately 9.5 percent of adult Americans are veterans.

ROCK STARS

The huge sculptures of Confederates Robert E. Lee, Jefferson Davis, and Stonewall Jackson carved into the side of Stone Mountain, Georgia, relied on major funding from the Ku Klux Klan (KKK).

Gutzon de la Mothe Borglum, the sculptor behind Mount Rushmore and Stone Mountain, was a member of the KKK.

TAKING ITS TOLL

The state of Texas has the most toll facilities—fifty-one. New Jersey has the second most, with forty, followed by New York with thirty-seven, Florida with thirty-four, and California with eighteen.

TAKE ME HOME

West Virginia has the nation's highest home ownership rate at 73 percent. New York State has the lowest rate, with 53 percent.

LOTTO FEVER

Lotteries in America paid out $40 billion in 2011, but $800 million in prize money remained unclaimed.

WEATHER YOU LIKE IT OR NOT

2011 was the twenty-third warmest year on record in the United States.

In 2011, Indiana, Kentucky, Massachusetts, New Jersey, New York, Ohio, and Pennsylvania had their wettest year since records were first kept in 1895. Texas had its driest year on record.

More than five hundred people died from tornadoes in the United States in 2011, compared to only twenty-six who were killed by lightning. In the 1940s, an average of about four hundred people died from lightning strikes each year.

About 10 percent of people struck by lightning actually die.

December is the month with the fewest thunderstorms in the United States.

2012 set an all-time record low for the number of tornadoes in the United States—about 1,072 reported and 919 confirmed. There were about 1,500 in 2011. The average year has about 1,200 twisters.

The record low temperature for the lower forty-eight states is −33°F at Soda Butte, Wyoming, on October 29, 1917.

Roughly 60 percent of the storms that enter the United States do so through the Pacific Northwest.

UNITED STOUTS OF AMERICA

West Virginia is the state with the highest obesity rate in the country—34.3 percent—followed closely by Delaware and Mississippi.

Colorado had the lowest obesity rate—20.1 percent— followed by Utah and Connecticut.

One in three American homeless people is obese.

ONE FOR THE ROAD

One in six American adults is a binge drinker, consuming an average of eight drinks per session, and doing so four times a month. Most drunk drivers are binge drinkers.

Some 23 percent of men binge drink, as compared to 11.4 percent of women.

Most binge drinkers are not alcoholics.

HOT WHEELS

The most-stolen cars in America are, in order, the Honda Accord, Honda Civic, Toyota Camry, Acura Integra, and Cadillac Escalade.

KNOT FOR EVERYONE

In 2011, 51 percent of American adults were married. That compares to 72 percent in 1960.

Just 20 percent of Americans aged eighteen to twenty-nine were married in 2011, compared with 59 percent in 1960.

June is the most popular month in the United States to get married, followed by September and October. The least popular month to tie the knot is January, followed by February and March.

The South has the highest U.S. divorce rate. The Northeast has the lowest rate.

BABY BLUES

There were 10 million single mothers in the United States in 2011, up from 8.4 million in 1990 and 3.4 million in 1970.

> In 2010, the teen birth rate in the United States reached its lowest level since data have been collected—34.3 births per one thousand teenage girls aged fifteen to nineteen. The teen pregnancy rate has dropped 44 percent since peaking in 1991.

There were 1,735,000 American single fathers raising children under the age of eighteen in 2011. This is up from 393,000 in 1970 and 1,351,000 in 1990.

SEEING DOUBLE

The number of twin births in America more than doubled between 1980 and 2009, going from 1.9 percent of births to 3.3 percent. The rate of twin births for mothers over forty increased by over 200 percent. The increase was attributed to increased use of fertility treatments and older maternal age.

INCARCERATION NATION

Nearly one in three Americans will have been arrested by the time he or she is twenty-three.

As of late 2012, three hundred prisoners on death row in America had had their sentences overturned based on DNA evidence that showed they did not commit the crime.

Roughly ten thousand prisoners a year have their sentences reduced because they cooperated with law enforcement officials by providing incriminating information about others.

American prisons, by and large, ban inmates from having dental floss for various reasons, including:

- In Texas, a prisoner used dental floss and toothpaste to saw through the bars of his cell.

- In Illinois, Maryland, West Virginia, and Wisconsin, inmates saved enough dental floss to braid into rope and used it to try and climb over prison walls.

- An Illinois prisoner used floss to stitch together the dummy he left behind in his bed when he took off.

HOLIDAY RUSH

Fourteen percent of Americans begin decorating for Christmas on Thanksgiving or earlier. Thirty percent do so the day after Thanksgiving. Two percent wait until Christmas Eve.

There were 190 home fires started by Christmas trees in 2009, down from 850 in 1980.

According to *AdWeek*, the top ten shoplifted items at Christmastime 2011 were filet mignon, high-end liquors, power tools, the iPhone 4, Gillette Mach 4 razors, Axe scented products, designer clothes, Let's Rock Elmo, high-end perfumes, and Nikes, in that order.

YOUR TAX DOLLARS AT WORK

Some of the more curious expenditures made by the U.S. Congress in 2011 include $10 million to remake *Sesame Street* for Pakistani audiences, $764,825 to study how college students use mobile devices for social networking, and $550,000 to study how rock music contributed to the downfall of the Soviet Union.

In fiscal years 2010 and 2011, the U.S. Department of Agriculture spent $2 million on an intern program that only hired one person.

SMASHING THE GLASS CEILING

Some notable women CEOs of major American corporations in 2012 included Irene Rosenfeld of Kraft, Ellen Kullman of DuPont, Lynn Elsenhans of Sunoco, Indra Nooyi of PepsiCo, Ursula Burns of Xerox, Meg Whitman of Hewlett-Packard, Denise Morrison of Campbell Soup, Marillyn Hewson of Lockheed Martin, and Virginia Rometty of IBM.

JOINT DECISION

About 50 percent of Americans surveyed say that marijuana should be legalized.

DOWNER DATA

Health.com conducted a 2011 study of federal health data and determined that the ten states with the greatest percentages of depressed people were, in alphabetical order: Arkansas, Indiana, Kentucky, Michigan, Mississippi, Missouri, Nevada, Oklahoma, Tennessee, and West Virginia.

LUXURIOUS LISTINGS

The most expensive apartment in New York was sold in 2011 for $88 million. A Citigroup executive sold the penthouse on Central Park West to Dmitry Rybolovlev, a Russian fertilizer magnate, who bought it so his daughter would have a place to stay while attending college in the United States.

The most expensive American residential real estate transaction of 2011 was the sale of a 25,000-square-foot Palo Alto, California, mansion known as Loire Chateau. It was purchased by Russian billionaire venture capitalist Yuri Milner for $100 million as a vacation home.

SQUEEZE INN

The thinnest house in New York City is the famed home at 75½ Bedford Street, which is just nine and a half feet wide. The 990-square-foot dwelling's occupants over the years have included Cary Grant, John Barrymore, and Margaret Mead.

GONE TO THE DOGS

About 55 percent of people sleep with their dogs, 55 percent buy them holiday gifts, and 40 percent take them on vacation.

YOU CAN'T EAT THAT

The sale of the pear-shaped fruit ackee—the national fruit of Jamaica—is banned in the United States, as it contains toxins that can restrict the body's ability to release sugar, causing the blood sugar level to drop and potentially resulting in death.

Eating horsemeat is legal in most states, but killing a horse for its meat is illegal throughout the country.

The sale of unpasteurized, or raw, milk is banned in twenty-one states.

Wild beluga caviar from the Black Sea and Caspian Sea basins has been banned in the United States since 2005 because the beluga is a threatened species.

Durian is known as the "king of fruits" in Asia, but has a disgusting smell that many people find revolting. Because of its horrific odor, the public consumption of durian is illegal in some Asian cities and it is extremely hard to find in the United States.

The sale of redfish was been banned in all states except Mississippi since 1986. The fish population was decimated after famous chef Paul Prudhomme popularized blackened redfish. The U.S. Commerce Department has since shut down redfish fisheries.

Foie gras, the livers from force-fed ducks and geese, is illegal in most of Europe. Only France, Belgium, Hungary, Bulgaria, and Spain still allow its production. The state of California and the city of Chicago have also banned its sale.

SHIPPING NEWS

The busiest port in the United States in 2010 was South Louisiana, which handled 236 million tons of cargo. The next four busiest ports were Houston, Texas; New York/New Jersey; Beaumont, Texas; and Long Beach, California.

STRIP SEARCH

The Las Vegas Strip is not in Las Vegas. The 4.2-mile stretch of Las Vegas Boulevard South runs through Paradise, Nevada, and Winchester, Nevada, which lie just south of Las Vegas proper.

Fifteen of the world's largest twenty-five hotels are located on the Strip.

MY OLD KENTUCKY HOME

Half of what is now Kentucky was known as the Transylvania Colony in 1775, after the land was purchased from the Cherokee tribe by Richard Henderson, owner of the Transylvania Company. A year later, the sale of the land, which belonged to North Carolina and Virginia, was invalidated by the Virginia General Assembly. (*Transylvania* means "after the woods" in Latin.)

Henderson is the man who hired Daniel Boone to blaze the Wilderness Road and the Cumberland Gap to open the way for settlement of the area.

Seventeen and a half square miles of western Kentucky lies outside the rest of the state in what is known as the Kentucky Bend, enclosed in an oxbow loop on the Mississippi River and surrounded by Missouri and Tennessee. There are but seventeen people living in this area and their mailing address is Tiptonville, Tennessee.

NATIONAL GEOGRAPHIC

The area encompassing present-day West Virginia and western Pennsylvania was originally proposed to be the fourteenth state of the Union and would have been called Westsylvania. Congress nixed the idea in 1776.

When surveyors laid down the border between Tennessee and Georgia, they were off by about a mile, erring in the favor of Tennessee. Since then, Tennessee has had fifty-one square miles of land that should have been in Georgia. Nine times since 1890, Georgia has petitioned Tennessee to give the land back, to no avail.

Ten states border the Mississippi River.

Some of the Florida Panhandle is in the Central Time Zone, while the rest of the state is in the Eastern Time Zone.

The Appalachian Mountains run through eighteen states.

The arc on Delaware's northern border is known as the twelve-mile circle. The arc has existed since the Duke of York ceded Delaware to William Penn in 1682 and specified that the northern border be a compass arc drawn twelve miles from the cupola on the old New Castle Courthouse.

LAWS OF THE LAND

Nearly forty thousand new state laws were enacted across the USA in 2011.

In 1790, there were twenty federal laws on the books. Now there are about 4,500. No one knows the exact number.

Some unusual state laws follow:

In Alabama, it is illegal to wrestle a bear.

In Alaska, one needs an elephant permit to import or export an elephant.

In Arizona, it's a crime to leave a fishing rod unattended.

In Arkansas, it is illegal for a pinball machine to give more than twenty-five free games to a high scorer.

In California, home sellers must warn buyers if the house is believed to be haunted.

In Colorado, it is illegal to duel.

In Connecticut, the cutting down of a tree to catch a raccoon is illegal.

In Delaware, it is illegal to sell dog hair.

In Florida, it is illegal for a woman to fall asleep under a hair dryer.

In Georgia, it is illegal to sell a child off to the circus.

In Hawaii, it's a crime to have more than fifteen cats or dogs in a household.

In Idaho, cannibalism is prohibited, except in life-or-death situations.

In Illinois, a motorcyclist can now go through a red light if the motorist feels the light has been red a "reasonable length of time."

In Indiana, it is illegal to display the alcohol content of a beer on the label.

In Iowa, it is a crime for parents to display their deformed children in the circus.

In Kansas, it is illegal to kill a cow with a hammer.

In Kentucky, it is a crime for a driver to coast down a hill.

In Louisiana, it is illegal for spectators at a sporting event to insult the players.

In Maine, it is against the law to advertise on a rock.

In Maryland, it is illegal to have more than three turtles.

In Massachusetts, it is unlawful to possess an explosive golf ball.

In Michigan, it is illegal to only play part of the national anthem.

In Minnesota, only the blind may possess a white cane.

In Mississippi, it is a crime to use vulgar language in the presence of two or more people.

In Missouri, it is against the law to fake blindness to make money.

In Montana, it is unlawful to drive animals onto a railway to stop a train.

In Nebraska, doing a reverse bungee jump is illegal.

In Nevada, cursing in front of a corpse is against the law.

In New Hampshire, it is illegal to work or play on Sunday, except out of necessity.

In New Jersey, it is against the law to detain a homing pigeon.

In New Mexico, it is illegal to trip a horse.

In New York, it is a crime to sell cat fur.

In North Carolina, it is unlawful to sing off key.

In North Dakota, kangaroo boxing is prohibited.

In Ohio, it is illegal for horses to copulate within thirty feet of a public road.

In Oklahoma, it's against the law to bet on elections.

In Oregon, it is unlawful to strap a child to the hood, fender, or roof of a car.

In Pennsylvania, a fortune-teller can't tell someone where to dig for buried treasure or try to shorten someone's life.

In Rhode Island, it's illegal to wrap just-caught fish in newspaper.

In South Carolina, it a crime to wear a mask in public, unless for a holiday or theatrical production.

In South Dakota, dogs cannot be used to hunt big game, except mountain lions.

In Tennessee, atheists are banned from holding public office.

In Texas, it is unlawful to fish off a bridge.

In Utah, it's illegal to cause a catastrophe.

In Vermont, it is a crime to sell dogs from the side of the road.

In Virginia, it is unlawful to write a term paper for someone else.

In Washington, it's illegal to attach a vending machine to a utility pole.

In West Virginia, it's against the law to ski while drunk.

In Wisconsin, livestock have the right of way along roads.

In Wyoming, it's against the law to fish using corn for bait.

COMMERCE CLAUSE

The State of Alabama has a ten-cent sales tax on decks of cards and charges retailers a one- to three-dollar license tax for selling them.

Fat Bastard wine can be sold in Alabama, but Dirty Bastard beer is illegal because its name is considered profane.

SUPERSIZE IT

The 180,000-square-foot Longaberger Basket Company Building in Newark, Ohio, is a giant replica of an actual Longaberger basket.

The parking garage of the Kansas City Public Library in Missouri has a facade that is a replica of a giant bookshelf, featuring the bindings of giant books relevant to the city.

TAKE IT TO THE BANK, OR NOT

Ten million American households have no checking or savings account. Mississippi, which has the highest poverty rate in the United States, also has the highest percentage of "unbanked" people—15 percent. New Hampshire, which has the lowest poverty rate, has the lowest number of "unbanked" people—1.9 percent.

WILL THAT BE CASH OR CREDIT?

As of late 2012, an average American family's share of the national debt was $137,000.

The first American one-dollar bill, issued in 1862, featured a portrait of Salmon P. Chase, the secretary of the treasury. George Washington and Christopher Columbus replaced Chase in 1869. The front (obverse) side design used today was introduced in 1963.

It would take 1.8 trillion pennies to fill the Empire State Building.

I CAN'T DRIVE 85

Texas Highway 130, which links Austin to San Antonio, raised its speed limit to 85 miles per hour in 2012, making it the fastest stretch of road in the United States. In October 2012, a motorist on the road was pulled over for driving 225 miles per hour.

FLAG FALLACY

Contrary to popular misconception, an American flag that touches the ground is not required to be burned.

MICKEY D'S

McDonald's original menu featured barbeque sandwiches as the top seller. Hamburgers, chili tamales, and peanut butter and jelly sandwiches were also available.

Americans consume some 5.5 million cows' worth of beef each year at McDonald's.

McDonald's feeds 68 million people a day, or about 1 percent of the world population.

Jay Leno, Shania Twain, Pink, Rachel McAdams, and Sharon Stone all worked at McDonald's before making it big.

The Big Mac special sauce consists of the following: soybean oil, pickle relish [diced pickles, high fructose corn syrup, sugar, vinegar, corn syrup, salt, calcium chloride, xanthan gum, potassium sorbate (a preservative), spice extractives, polysorbate 80], distilled vinegar, water, egg yolks, high fructose corn syrup, onion powder, mustard seed, salt, spices, propylene glycol alginate, sodium benzoate (a preservative), mustard bran, sugar, garlic powder, vegetable protein (hydrolyzed corn, soy, and wheat), caramel color, extractives of paprika, soy lecithin, turmeric (a colorant), calcium disodium EDTA (to protect flavor).

Over the years, the Big Mac sauce recipe went through changes. By the late 2000s, company executives had decided to go back to the original formula. The only problem was, they'd lost it. Eventually, by consulting with their old ingredient suppliers, they were able to recreate it.

CLIP JOINT

New York hairstylist Ted Gibson gets $950 per haircut, making his the most expensive haircut in the world.

GRAND OLD TIME

The oldest amusement park in the United States is Lake Compounce Family Theme Park in Bristol, Connecticut, which opened in 1846. Other ancient parks include Cedar Point in Sandusky, Ohio (1870); Idlewild Park in Ligonier, Pennsylvania (1878); Sea Breeze Amusement Park in Rochester, New York (1879); and Dorney Park in Allentown, Pennsylvania (1884).

The White Horse Tavern, in Newport, Rhode Island, is the country's oldest restaurant. The building has housed an eatery since 1673, the White House Tavern since 1730.

Other old eateries include Fraunces Tavern, in New York City, opened in 1762; the Griswold Inn, in Essex, Connection opened in 1776; the Union Oyster House, in Boston, opened in 1826; and Antoine's Restaurant, in New Orleans, opened in 1840.

BLACKOUT

There has never been a black Republican congresswoman elected to the U.S. House of Representatives.

As of early 2013, there is only one black member of the U.S. Senate, Timothy Scott; he was appointed by South Carolina governor Nikki Haley to fill the seat vacated by Senator Jim DeMint's resignation.

Scott is only the seventh black senator ever and the first from the South since 1881.

MOW TOWN

There are forty thousand square miles of lawn in America.

THE OTHER GARDEN STATE

Mormons believe that the Garden of Eden was/is in Missouri. They also believe the second coming of Christ will occur in Missouri.

Mormon founder Joseph Smith Jr. got his start as a treasure hunter. He used magical "seeing stones" stuck inside a stovepipe hat to find buried treasure and lost items. It was one of these stones that he claimed to have used to find golden plates sent from God that he spent years translating. They are the basis of the Mormon religion.

L'CHAIM

There are 6.6 million Jews living in America. New York has the highest number, with 8.4 percent, followed by New Jersey; Washington, DC; Massachusetts; and Maryland.

BABY, I HATE YOUR NAME

The most hated baby names of 2012 in America, according to a survey of online message board postings, are as follows:

- For girls, Nevaeh (which is "heaven" spelled backwards), Destiny, Madison, Mackenzie, Addison, Gertrude, Kaitlyn, Makayla, Bertha, and Hope were the top ten.

- For boys, the winners/losers were Jayden, Brayden, Aiden, Kaden, Hunter, Hayden, Bentley, Tristan, Michael, and Jackson.

According to the same survey, the most liked baby names of 2012 were as follows:

- The top ten girl names for 2012 were Sophia, Emma, Olivia, Isabella, Ava, Lily, Zoe, Chloe, Mia, and Madison. Sophia has been number one for three straight years.

- The top ten boy names were Aiden, Jackson, Ethan, Liam, Mason, Noah, Lucas, Jacob, Jayden, and Jack. Aiden, which was also the third most hated boys name, has been number one for eight straight years.

FARE-LY OLD

Johnnie "Spider" Footman, a ninety-two-year-old New York City cabbie, has been on the job since FDR was president and was still working as of 2012.

COIN-OPS

In California (and Japan) eggs are sold in vending machines.

In Pennsylvania wine is sold in vending machines, but first you must swipe your driver's license, have your picture taken by the machine, and then blow into a Breathalyzer.

There's a Maine lobster vending game where for three dollars one gets fifteen seconds to grab with a mechanical claw a live lobster from a tank in the machine.

REGIONAL REMARKS

In Wisconsin a drinking fountain is called a "bubbler."

In Nebraska a lottery ticket is called a "pickle."

An edible mushroom in Kentucky and Tennessee is called a "dry-land fish."

A tadpole is known as a "pinkwink" on Cape Cod.

A "devil strip" in northeastern Ohio is the strip of grass between the street and sidewalk.

A heavy rain is known as a "fence-lifter" in the Ozarks, a "toad-strangler" in the Gulf States, and a "turd-floater" in Texas.

NEW YORK STATE OF MIND

New York is the most expensive American city in which to park a car. Monthly car park rates in midtown averaged $541 and downtown averaged $533, in 2012. Over the lifetime of an average car, that's roughly $71,000. Boston, San Francisco, Philadelphia, and Seattle round out the top five.

New York state residents pay the highest state and local taxes as a percentage of income, followed by New Jersey and Connecticut. Alaska, South Dakota, and Tennessee pay the lowest.

Riders board New York City subways 8.1 million times every weekday. The next closest system in ridership is the Washington, DC, Metro with 1 million boardings a day, followed by Chicago with 738,000, Boston with 539,000, and San Francisco with 393,000.

THE PLANE TRUTH

At the time of this writing, no passenger has died in a commercial plane crash in the United States since 2009. It has been more than ten years since the last fatal crash of a large jetliner in the United States.

Before 9/11, there were only thirty-three federal air marshals. Now there are thousands (the exact number is classified).

In 2011, the TSA (Transportation Security Administration) found 1,306 firearms in carry-on luggage.

AMERICAN WOMAN

Women buy 91 percent of romance novels. The average age of a print version romance novel reader is forty-nine.

Twenty-three percent of American gun owners are women.

Since 2000, 19 percent of married American women have kept their maiden names.

ALL IN A DAY'S WORK

Fifty percent of American workers buy coffee at work, spending an average of twenty dollars a week.

Sixty-six percent of workers buy lunch out, spending thirty-seven dollars a week on average. Men and younger workers spend the most.

WORKING MAN BLUES

Forty-one percent of men say navy blue is their favorite color to wear to work.

Fifty-one percent of women claim that black is their favorite color to wear to work.

CHECK IT OUT

The Library of Congress has 650 miles of shelves.

The Library of Congress houses more than 127,000 U.S. telephone directories.

There is a tunnel that connects the Library of Congress with the U.S. Capitol Building.

TRICK OR TREAT

Seventy-four percent of Americans say that they hand out candy on Halloween.

WOULD YOU LIKE FRIES WITH THAT?

In a 2012 study, Wendy's was found to have the fastest service of the major fast-food chains. The average wait time at a Wendy's was 129.75 seconds. This compares with Taco Bell at 149.69 seconds, McDonald's at 188.83, Chick-fil-A at 190.06, and Burger King at 201.33.

As far as accuracy goes, Chick-fil-A was found to correctly fill an order 92.4 percent of the time, compared with Taco Bell at 91.2 percent, McDonald's at 90.0 percent, Wendy's at 89.9 percent, and Burger King at 83 percent.

Chick-fil-A was ranked tops in friendliness.

CHURCH CHAT

In 2012, the Catholic Church canonized its first Native American—Kateri Tekakwitha—a Mohawk woman who lived in the seventeenth century.

The largest church stained-glass window is on the north side of the Cathedral Basilica of the Assumption in Covington, Kentucky. It measures twenty-four feet wide by sixty-seven feet high.

A greater percentage of Republicans attend church than do Democrats.

Pennsylvania has the largest Amish population of any state, followed by Ohio.

STREET SMART

The most common street name in the United States is Second. It's not First because what would have been First is often named Main or something similar, like Broadway.

American Realtors say the name of a street a home is on can have an influence on the speed of its sale. Names like Crummy Road (in Clark Fork, Idaho) or Butt Road (Fort Wayne, Indiana) can make it harder to sell a house on such a street.

BREW MASTERS

New Hampshire leads the nation in annual consumption of twelve-ounce beers per person with 459, followed by North Dakota at 450, Montana at 433, South Dakota at 405, and Nevada at 389.

TATT'S THE FACT

About 23 percent of women and 19 percent of men in the United States have tattoos.

TURKEY TIME

Contrary to common belief, the day before Thanksgiving is not the busiest travel day of the year. The busiest travel days are usually Fridays in June, July, and August.

Calls to plumbers double the day after Thanksgiving.

Illinois grows one-half the country's pumpkin crop.

Pumpkins sold for carving are no good for making pie. Smaller sugar pumpkins with a firm, sweet flesh are used in canned pumpkin pie filling.

Cranberries did not become associated with Thanksgiving until the early 1800s.

OIL CHANGE

The U.S. Department of Energy estimates that by 2020 America will be the world's biggest producer of oil, due to improved technologies, fracking, and more efficient energy use.

> The United States currently imports about 20 percent of its oil needs, but is expected to be self-sufficient by 2035.

MISSISSIPPI MUD

One home in Mississippi, valued at sixty-nine thousand dollars, had thirty-four different flood insurance claims between 1978 and 2012, totaling almost ten times the house's worth.

AND THE WINNER IS . . .

American presidential elections are decided by the electoral college, not by popular vote. One of the main reasons this odd situation came to be was that at the 1787 Constitutional Convention, a direct election did not sit well with the Southern slaveholding state delegates, whose states had large populations but far fewer eligible voters. The convention also agreed to count each slave as three-fifths of a person for calculating the states' allotment of seats in Congress and thus each state's electoral college votes.

Each state is allotted a number of electors equal to its number of representatives and senators in Congress.

In theory, the electors should vote for the candidate that wins their state, but twenty-one states have no legal requirement for them to do so. In these states, electors swear a nonbinding pledge to their party to vote for the winning candidate.

There have been numerous "faithless electors" over the years, notably in 1832 when all thirty Pennsylvania electors refused to vote for Democratic vice presidential candidate Martin Van Buren, and in 1836 when twenty-three Virginia voters refused to vote for Democratic vice presidential candidate Richard Mentor Johnson.

Washington, DC, is allotted the same number of electors it would have if it were a state, but it cannot have more than the least populous state.

During the 2012 presidential election, there were several wards in Philadelphia where Mitt Romney didn't receive one vote. In these wards, Barack Obama beat Romney 19,605 to zero.

When it comes to voter apathy, Hawaii is king. In the 2008 presidential election, Hawaii had the lowest turnout—only 48.8 percent of eligible voters did so, even though Barack Obama, who is from the state, was running. In 2012, Hawaii tied with West Virginia for lowest voter turnout—44.2 percent.

The state with the highest voter turnout in 2008 was Minnesota, at 77.8 percent. Washington State was the leader in 2012, at 81 percent.

Robert McDonald finished tied with another candidate for the final seat on the Walton City, Kentucky, City Council after the 2012 election. Both candidates finished with 669 votes. McDonald would have won outright if his wife had bothered to vote. He lost a subsequent coin toss that decided the winner.

WHERE DO YOU WANT TO EAT TONIGHT?

There are 980,000 eateries in the United States. They employ 10 percent of the American workforce.

THE WEST WING

MASTER AND COMMANDER

Thomas Jefferson didn't like to have his slaves beaten, but when he thought it "necessary," they would only be whipped on the arms and legs.

Jefferson only ever agreed to free five of his nearly 150 slaves. Not even on his deathbed would he relent.

William Henry Harrison had ten children with his wife and six with one of his African slaves, Dilsia. When he ran for president, he did not want his children with Dilsia around, so he gave them to his brother, who sold them into slavery.

Zachary Taylor was the last U.S. president to hold slaves while in office.

EXPAT EXPREZ

John Tyler is the only president who was not a U.S. citizen when he died. He passed away while living in Virginia, during the Civil War, which was part of the Confederate States of America at the time.

John Tyler was elected to the Confederate House of Representatives after serving as president.

YOU CAN'T WIN THEM ALL

Millard Fillmore ran for president again four years after his first term ended. He got 21.6 percent of the popular vote as a third party candidate for the Know Nothing Party. (Membership in the Know Nothings was limited to Protestant men over the age of twenty-one and of British lineage. They were opposed to the influx of Irish and German Catholics into America.)

Ulysses S. Grant tried to run for a third term as president, but didn't receive enough votes at the 1880 Republican Convention.

In 1912, Teddy Roosevelt helped form the Progressive Party, also known as the "Bull Moose Party," after he was denied the Republican nomination that year. The party got its name after a reporter asked about Teddy's health and was told, "I am as fit as a bull moose."

William Howard Taft was the only incumbent president who ran for reelection and came in third.

Richard Nixon lost his first election, that for president of his high school class.

SLACKER-IN-CHIEF

Franklin Pierce had the worst grades in his class during his sophomore year in college.

James Buchanan was expelled from college.

Franklin Delano Roosevelt (FDR) was a C student while at Harvard.

Woodrow Wilson did not learn to read until after he was ten.

Harry Truman was the last president who did not have a college degree.

LEARNED LEADERS

Andrew Johnson taught himself how to read and write. His wife taught him arithmetic.

Starting at age eleven, John Quincy Adams kept a diary that reached fifty volumes by the time of his death.

Rutherford B. Hayes was the valedictorian of his college class.

George W. Bush was the only president with an MBA, which he earned at Harvard.

Theodore Roosevelt was a published ornithologist. He read several books a day in many different languages.

AFFLUENT ABE

Abraham Lincoln may have been born in a log cabin in Kentucky, but his father was in the top 15 percent of tax-paying property owners in his community.

PRESIDENTIAL PRECURSORS

James Garfield was a preacher before becoming president.

Benjamin Harrison once was a town crier for the federal court in Indianapolis, walking the streets and declaring announcements from the court. The job paid $2.50 a day.

Harry S. Truman once worked as a railroad timekeeper, sleeping in hobo camps near the line. He also worked in the mailroom of the *Kansas City Star* newspaper.

William Henry Harrison at one time ran a distillery, but closed the business out of concern for what liquor did to his customers.

Herbert Hoover had a degree in geology and worked as a mining engineer for many years.

John Fitzgerald Kennedy was the first former Boy Scout to become president.

Lyndon Baines Johnson was a teacher before entering politics.

Ronald Reagan was president of his college class.

Reagan began his career in show business broadcasting University of Iowa football games on the radio for ten dollars. He then moved on to announcing Chicago Cubs baseball games for a Des Moines, Iowa, radio station, doing play-by-play from accounts that came to the station over the newswire.

Reagan served several terms as president of the Screen Actors Guild.

Gerald Ford washed dishes to help pay his way through college.

When he lived in Indonesia, Barack Obama had a pet ape named Tata.

As a teenager, Obama worked at a Baskin-Robbins. He now claims to dislike ice cream.

Bill Clinton sang in a chorus and played rugby in his younger days.

George W. Bush was head cheerleader at the all-male private boarding school he attended.

Like Bill Clinton, George W. Bush played rugby in college.

AFTERTHOUGHTS

William Howard Taft, who was appointed chief justice of the U.S. Supreme Court after he left office, was the only former president to have administered the oath of office to another president and sit on the high bench with other justices that he had appointed.

Andrew Johnson served in the U.S. Senate after he left the White House. He is the only former president to do so.

After he left office, Ulysses S. Grant lost all his money to a swindler he had invested with. William Vanderbilt bailed Grant out with a $150,000 loan.

After leaving the White House, Theodore Roosevelt went on an African safari to collect specimens for the Smithsonian Institution and the American Museum of Natural History. His hunting party killed some 11,397 animals of all types and sizes. (Roosevelt loved to kill animals, study, and stuff them. At a young age, he had his own little museum from his collection.)

THE SPORTING LIFE

Woodrow Wilson was the first president to throw out an opening pitch at a World Series baseball game and the first to watch a movie in the White House: *The Birth of a Nation.*

> Wilson holds the record for rounds of golf played by a president while in office—one thousand. He would have the Secret Service agents paint his golf balls black so he could find them while playing golf in the snow outside the White House.

Teddy Roosevelt came in second in the Harvard boxing championship.

> George H. W. Bush was the captain of the Yale baseball team and played in the first two College World Series.

Gerald Ford was the starting center and linebacker on the 1932 and 1933 Michigan football teams that won national championships. After graduation, both the Detroit Lions and the Green Bay Packers offered Ford contracts.

CALL OF DUTY

Calvin Coolidge was initially sworn into office as president after President Harding's sudden death in 1923, by his father, who was a notary public, at 2:37 a.m. He took the oath and promptly went back to bed. He was later sworn in by a judge.

LBJ was the first president sworn into office by a woman—federal judge Sarah T. Hughes, aboard Air Force One, two hours and eight minutes after JFK was assassinated.

There was no Bible with which to swear in Johnson, so a Roman Catholic missal found on the plane was used instead.

HEROIC HOOVER

Herbert Hoover is credited by some as having saved more people than any other person in history, when the relief agency he headed provided food to 10.5 million Russians during the Russian Famine of 1921–23, one of the greatest human disasters in Europe since the Black Death.

Herbert Hoover was the first president born west of the Mississippi River, in Iowa.

HIGH SCHOOL HIGH JINX

John F. Kennedy blew up a toilet at his private high school.

Barack Obama's high school yearbook picture has the inscription "Thanks Tut, Gramps, Choom Gang, and Ray for all the good times." "Choom" was the local slang term for marijuana. His pot-smoking buddies were the Choom Gang.

NIX THAT IDEA

Richard Nixon applied for a job at the FBI. He was actually accepted, but due to budget cuts, he was never hired.

Nixon was turned away by two Manhattan apartment buildings in 1980 before finally buying a co-op. He later moved to a home in New Jersey.

MELTDOWN MAN

While serving in the U.S. Navy, Jimmy Carter helped to dismantle a nuclear reactor that had melted down. Along with others, he took turns being lowered into the reactor in a special suit for a few minutes at a time to disassemble the unit.

Carter taught Sunday school throughout his life.

ALSO RANS

In high school, Sarah Palin led her basketball team to the state title and was known as "Sarah the Barracuda."

In high school, Mitt Romney was on the pep squad and the glee club and was manager of the hockey team and chairman of the homecoming committee.

Al Gore is worth $300 million. That's $80 million more than Mitt Romney is worth.

KILLING LINCOLN

Major Henry Reed Rathbone and his fiancée, Clara Harris, were present with Abraham and Mary Lincoln in the box at Ford's Theatre the night the president was shot. Rathbone struggled with Lincoln's assassin, John Wilkes Booth, as Booth tried to jump from the box to the stage, and was severely injured by knife wounds from Booth in the process.

> Rathbone was never mentally stable after the assassination and later killed Clara, his wife, with a knife and stabbed himself in a suicide attempt.

The National Museum of Health and Medicine in Silver Springs, Maryland, houses the bullet that killed Lincoln and a fragment of his skull.

> The museum collection, which contains 25 million objects, also features a piece of President James Garfield's spine and the bullet that pierced it when fired by Charles Guiteau. Guiteau's brain is also on display.

PRESIDENTIAL PREROGATIVE

Since 1881, American presidents have vetoed an average of one bill every twenty days.

Grover Cleveland had the highest veto average—one every five days.

Barack Obama had the lowest average in his first term—one every 490 days.

George W. Bush averaged one every 244 days.

FDR vetoed one bill every seven days.

NO JUSTICE

Only four U.S. presidents didn't get to make any appointments to the U.S. Supreme Court—William Henry Harrison, Zachary Taylor, Andrew Johnson, and Jimmy Carter. Carter was the only one of the four to serve a full term.

George Washington appointed ten justices and FDR appointed eight.

Ronald Reagan appointed the most federal judges of any president—376.

THREESOMES

Twice in American history three presidents have served in the same calendar year. The first time was in 1841, when William Henry Harrison succeeded Martin Van Buren and then died thirty days into his office, making way for John Tyler to occupy the Oval Office. The second time was in 1881, when Rutherford B. Hayes was succeeded by James Garfield, who was assassinated and replaced by Chester A. Arthur.

TRAINS, PLANES, AND AUTOMOBILES

Air Force One (the president's plane) costs $179,750 an hour to operate.

> FDR had a secret train terminal built deep beneath Grand Central Station in New York, so he could enter and leave the city without the public becoming aware that he was crippled from polio. The terminal still exists today and is heavily guarded and at the ready if a visiting president needs to make a quick, covert exit from the Big Apple.

FDR used an armored car confiscated from Al Capone by the Treasury Department when he was driven from the White House to give his "Day of Infamy" speech before Congress after the Japanese attack on Pearl Harbor. There were rumors that Japanese assassins would attack him, but there was no money in the budget for an armored car for the president.

> The hearse that carried President John F. Kennedy after his assassination sold for $160,000 at auction.

A sixteen-cylinder Cadillac convertible, used as a presidential parade limousine by Franklin D. Roosevelt, sold for $270,000.

HOW LOW CAN YOU GO?

Politics today may be dirty, but it pales in comparison to elections of the past:

- The election of 1800 pitted President Thomas Jefferson against Vice President John Adams. Jefferson wrote that Adams was a "hideous hermaphroditical character which has neither the force and firmness of a man, nor the gentleness and sensibility of a woman." Adams countered with "Are you prepared to see your dwellings in flames . . . female chastity violated . . . children writhing on the pike? Great God of compassion and justice, shield my country from destruction."

- In the election of 1828, between President John Quincy Adams and Andrew Jackson, accusations flew that Jackson was a murderer and an adulterer and that his wife was a bigamist, who was a "dirty black wench" and prone to "open and notorious lewdness."

- Adams was accused of serving as a pimp to the czar of Russia for providing his wife's maid as a concubine and of having a government-funded billiard table in the White House. Jackson won the election, and his wife Rachel died before the inauguration from the stress of the campaign. Jackson blamed his enemies for her death and refused to meet the outgoing President Adams as was customary, and Adams refused to attend Jackson's inauguration.

- In the 1860 election between Stephen Douglas and Abraham Lincoln, Douglas called Lincoln a "horrid-looking wretch, sooty and scoundrelly in aspect, a cross between the nutmeg dealer, the horse-swapper and the nightman," as well as the "leanest, lankest, most ungainly mass of legs and arms and hatchet face ever strung on a single frame." Lincoln, for his part, referred to Douglas as "about five feet nothing in height and about the same in diameter the other way."

- In 1928, Herbert Hoover faced Catholic New York governor Al Smith. The Holland Tunnel was just being completed at the time, and Hoover supporters claimed that the tunnel would go all the way to the Vatican and that the pope would have a say in all presidential decisions if Smith were elected.

FIRST FOIBLES

Bill Clinton has admitted to having adulterous affairs with Monica Lewinsky and Gennifer Flowers. Numerous other women have accused him of sexual harassment or rape. He paid Paula Jones $850,000 to settle a sexual harassment lawsuit she had brought against him.

In 1976, George W. Bush lost his driver's license for two years because of a DUI conviction.

PRESIDENTIAL PERIL

In 1776, future president James Monroe was shot in the shoulder during the Battle of Trenton. Surgeons could not remove the bullet. In 1785, during a visit to Mississippi, Monroe contracted malaria, from which he would suffer recurring bouts for the rest of his life. In 1830, he developed what is thought to have been tuberculois and died the next year.

In 1841, William Henry Harrison developed pneumonia after giving his inauguration speech in the rain. The lack of heating in the White House may have contributued to his death thirty days later.

While president, Teddy Roosevelt boxed regularly in the White House, until a sparring partner detached his left retina. He also liked to skinny-dip in the Potomac during the winter.

Just before he was inaugurated president, Franklin Pierce, his wife, and his son were in a terrible train wreck in which Benjamin, his only living son, was decapitated in front of him.

Pierce was an alcoholic.

William Howard Taft was known as "Big Bill," because of his insatiable appetite and severe obesity. This condition caused him to belch and fart uncontrollably at times.

In 1924, from playing tennis on the White House courts, Calvin Coolidge's son, Calvin Coolidge Jr., developed a blister that became infected, killing him within days.

William McKinley was shot by Leon Czolgosz at the Pan-American Exposition in Buffalo, New York. He was hit twice, and doctors were unable to find the second bullet in his body. Ironically, a new invention—the X-ray machine—was on exhibit at the exposition, but doctors were afraid to use it because they feared it might have adverse side effects.

Warren G. Harding had a nervous breakdown when he was twenty-four, and convalesced at the Battle Creek Sanatorium, run by the Kellogg brothers of cereal fame.

Woodrow Wilson suffered a stroke in 1896 that left him unable to write for a year. He suffered numerous smaller strokes after that, and a massive one in 1919 left him blind in one eye and wheelchair-bound.

FDR could not walk without assistance from 1921 until his death in 1945. He was terrified of being left alone, in case there was a fire and he could not escape.

Dwight David Eisenhower smoked four packs of cigarettes a day, until his doctors told him to stop. He quit cold turkey.

President Obama suffered a split lip from an elbow to the face delivered during a pickup basketball game in 2010. He required twelve stitches.

In 1997, President Bill Clinton fell down a flight of steps and needed a two-hour surgery to repair a damaged tendon in his leg.

As a teenager, Andrew Jackson acquired a scar on his hand and head from the sword of a British officer whom Jackson refused to polish the boots of while imprisoned by the British during the Revolutionary War. He also contracted smallpox while held by the British.

In 1844, President John Tyler was almost killed when the biggest naval gun at the time, known as the "Peacemaker," exploded while he was onboard the USS *Princeton*. The accident killed the secretary of state, the secretary of the navy, several dignitaries, and Tyler's slave.

DEPARTURE DEPARTMENT

James Monroe was the third president in a row to die on the Fourth of July, in 1831. John Adams and Thomas Jefferson had died exactly five years earlier.

In 1848, John Quincy Adams, who was a member of Congress at the time, collapsed on the floor of the House of Representatives due to a massive cerebral hemorrhage. He was taken to the House speaker's office inside the Capitol Building and died there two days later.

John Quincy Adams lived long enough to know both the Founding Fathers and Abraham Lincoln.

John Tyler is buried next to James Monroe in Richmond, Virginia.

Calvin Coolidge was born on July 4, 1872. He is the only president to have been born on Independence Day.

Just before his death, Chester Arthur had almost all of his personal and professional papers burned.

Woodrow Wilson, who was buried at the National Cathedral, is the only U.S. president interred in Washington, DC.

Ulysses S. Grant's Tomb in Riverside Park, New York, is the largest mausoleum in North America.

After his death, Congress granted William Henry Harrison's wife a payment of $25,000 and the right to mail letters for free.

FDR had a very close relationship with his secretary Marguerite "Missy" LeHand and his will stipulated that she would get half the income from his estate if he died before her. Sadly, she attempted suicide in 1941, a few weeks after Roosevelt became close to Princess Martha of Norway and distanced himself from her.

Lyndon Johnson died at the age of sixty-four from a heart attack, on January 22, 1973, the day before the peace treaty ending the Vietnam War was signed.

Gerald Ford lived the longest of any U.S. president—ninety-three years and 165 days, besting Ronald Reagan by forty-five days.

YAK ATTACK

While modern-day U.S. presidents speak to the public almost daily, either directly or through surrogates, chief executives in the old days pretty much remained silent. George Washington averaged just three public speeches a year, John Adams and Andrew Jackson only one, and James Madison zero.

Calvin Coolidge had a very outgoing wife, and he was rather quiet in social settings, leading to his nickname "Silent Cal." Although perceived as quiet, with a retiring nature, Coolidge actually gave more press conferences—529—than any other president.

Dorothy Parker once said to Coolidge, "Mr. Coolidge, I've made a bet against a fellow who said it was impossible to get more than two words out of you." Coolidge famously replied, "You lose." When Parker heard years later that Coolidge had died, she replied, "How can they tell?"

ALL IN THE FAMILY

George Washington never had any biological children. It is believed that he was sterile.

> Washington married Martha Dandridge Custis, a wealthy widow who had four children from her first marriage, and he raised her two surviving kids as his own.

Washington had only met with Martha one or two times before asking for her hand.

> John Adams married his third cousin Abigail Smith.

John Adams's second cousin was Founding Father Samuel Adams (who has no connection with Samuel Adams beer).

> Just like George Washington, Thomas Jefferson married a widow named Martha—Martha Wayles Skelton.

Jefferson's slave, Sally Hemings, who historians believe had a sexual relationship with him, was a half-sister of Martha's, being her father's daughter.

> Only two of Jefferson's six children lived to adulthood.

James Madison had eleven siblings.

As a child, Madison was known as "Jemmy."

Madison was forty-three when he married widow Dolley Payne Todd. As Madison was not a Quaker and Dolley was, she was expelled from the religion.

John Quincy Adams was named for his mother's maternal grandfather, Colonel John Quincy, for whom the town of Quincy, Massachusetts, was named.

John Quincy Adams married London-born Louisa Catherine Johnson. She was the only foreign-born first lady in U.S. history. Adams first met Johnson when he was twelve and she was four.

Martin Van Buren married his first cousin once removed, Hannah Hoes.

Declaration of Independence signer Benjamin Harrison was the father of President William Henry Harrison.

William Henry Harrison's grandson Benjamin Harrison was elected president in 1888.

Chester A. Arthur was named Chester after the doctor and family friend who delivered him.

Some questioned Arthur's eligibility to become president, as his father and mother lived in Canada on and off in the years before he was born in 1829. These nineteenth-century "birthers" never were able to disprove that Arthur was born in northern Vermont.

As of 2012, there were two of President John Tyler's grandsons still alive. Tyler was the tenth president, serving from 1841 to 1845.

A minister refused to baptize James Polk when his father refused to recognize Christianity.

Polk, who fathered no children, was probably sterile due to an operation to remove urinary stones when he was a young man.

Grover Cleveland was the only president to get married in the White House. His twenty-one-year-old bride, Frances Folsom, was the youngest first lady ever.

Zachary Taylor's son was a Confederate general and Taylor's brother was a Union general in the Civil War.

James Madison was Zachary Taylor's second cousin.

After his wife's death Benjamin Harrison married her niece. She was twenty-five years younger than him. His two adult children disapproved of the match and refused to attend the wedding.

As a child, William McKinley was known as "Wobbly Willie."

Former first lady Barbara Pierce Bush is a distant cousin of Franklin Pierce.

Theodore Roosevelt's childhood nickname was "Teedie."

Teddy Roosevelt stood in for his niece Eleanor's father at her wedding to Franklin Delano Roosevelt.

Teddy had a son named Kermit.

William Howard Taft's father, Alphonso, cofounded the Yale Skull and Bones secret society in 1832.

Woodrow Wilson's parents were Joseph Ruggles Wilson and Jessie Janet Woodrow.

James Buchanan was engaged in 1819, but his fiancée died, some believe from a drug overdose, shortly after rumors of his seeing other women began to circulate.

Buchanan never married, but lived with another man—Alabama senator Rufus King—for the fifteen years before he was elected president. Many believe the two were gay.

James Garfield's father was a wrestler.

William G. Harding married the daughter of his archrival, Florence Kling DeWolfe. Her father was so incensed at the wedding that he didn't speak to either one of them for eight years.

The first time Harry S. Truman proposed to future wife Bess, she turned him down.

Dwight D. Eisenhower's family name when his ancestors lived in Germany was Eisenhauer, meaning "iron miner." The name got misspelled when they came to the United States.

Eisenhower was one of seven boys, each of whom was given the nickname "Ike." One was called "Big Ike," one "Little Ike," and Dwight was known as "Ugly Ike."

Eisenhower was born David Dwight, but reversed the order of his names when he entered the U.S. Military Academy at West Point.

Eisenhower's second son, John Sheldon Doud Eisenhower, graduated from West Point on D-Day, June 6, 1944.

Eisenhower's mother was a Jehovah's Witness.

Jimmy Carter is a cousin of June Carter Cash and a distant cousin to Motown Records founder Berry Gordy Jr.

Jackie Kennedy's first pregnancy ended in miscarriage, her second with the baby being stillborn, and the couple's first surviving child died as a newborn.

Lady Bird Johnson was born Claudia Alta Taylor. Her nursemaid was the first to call her "Ladybird," after the beetle. While her father called her "Lady," LBJ called her "Bird."

Richard Nixon met Pat Ryan while the two were performing in a community theater. She rebuffed his advances numerous times before agreeing to date him.

Before marrying Pat, Richard Nixon was engaged to another woman, but it didn't work out.

Gerald R. Ford was born Leslie Lynch King Jr. on July 14, 1913. Ford's mother left his father sixteen days later, after he threatened to kill her and Ford with a butcher's knife.

Two years later, Ford's mother married Gerald Rudolff Ford and the couple began calling the future president Gerald Rudolff Ford Jr. Ford didn't officially change his name until 1935.

Ford didn't find out about his biological father or his half-siblings through King until he was seventeen.

Ford married Elizabeth "Betty" Bloomer Warren, a divorced ex-dancer.

Ronald Reagan is the only president who was divorced.

Actor William Holden was best man at Reagan's second marriage, to Nancy Davis.

Even while president, Reagan called Nancy "Mommy."

George and Barbara Bush are the longest-married first couple, having been married sixty-seven years as of 2012.

George W. Bush had a sister who died at the age of three from leukemia.

Barack Obama's father, who went to Hawaii from his native Kenya on a scholarship, never told Obama's mother that he was already married when they wed.

Obama's father left the family in Hawaii in 1963, when Barack was two, to study at Harvard. Obama only saw his father one more time before he died in 1985.

Obama's father died in a car accident.

In 1967, Obama's mother married Muslim Lolo Soetoro, who was from Indonesia.

SECOND BANANAS

As vice president, John Adams cast the tie-breaking vote in the Senate a record twenty-nine times.

> Thomas Jefferson's second vice president was George Clinton, who is no relation to Bill Clinton. Jefferson's attorney general was Levi Lincoln Sr., who was distantly related to Abraham Lincoln.

The first vice president to be invited to cabinet meetings was Calvin Coolidge, invited by Warren G. Harding.

> When Ronald Reagan ran for president, he first offered the position of vice president to Gerald Ford, who declined. George H. W. Bush was then chosen.

President George H. W. Bush considered Clint Eastwood as his running mate.

PICTURE THIS

James Monroe is pictured holding the flag in the famous painting *Washington Crossing the Delaware*.

WHAT IN THE WORLD?

FEELING A LITTLE IL

North Korea has the fourth-largest army in the world.

About one-quarter of North Korea's gross domestic product is spent on its military.

One can be executed in North Korea for making an international phone call or distributing Bibles. Public executions are held in stadiums, before thousands of spectators.

North Korea's late leader Kim Jong-il (1941–2011) had seventeen palaces throughout the country. He had live lobster airlifted to his personal train whenever he traveled outside North Korea. Citizens believed that he could control the weather by his mood, and he boasted of getting three or four holes-in-one whenever he golfed.

DOWN UNDER

There are about 1 million camels wandering Australia's deserts.

"Bluey" is a nickname for redheads in Australia.

The Dingo Fence, built between 1880 and 1885 to keep dingoes out of South Eastern Australia, is the longest fence in the world—at 3,488 miles.

Australia's Nullarbor Plain is the world's largest single piece of limestone—seventy-seven thousand square miles.

The longest straight railroad line in the world is 297 miles and is in the Nullarbor Plain.

SHOP TILL YOU DROP

The Dubai Mall, in the United Arab Emirates, is the largest shopping center in the world, boasting 1,200 stores and 160 eateries.

SEEING RED

There are twice as many cell phones in China as there are people in America.

135 million Chinese live on less than one dollar a day.

Seventy-seven percent of the world's pirated goods are made in China.

One-third of Chinese adults live with their parents.

Congestion on China's city streets is so bad that Beijing holds a lottery each month to assign twenty thousand license plates, out of a total of nine hundred thousand applications.

More than 30 million Chinese live in caves. They dig holes into soft soil in the sides of cliffs.

The Chinese spend 30 percent of their income on clothes. Americans spend 8 percent.

China has the world's largest graphite deposits and is the leading producer of pencils.

Cordyceps, a fungus that grows on worms, is a natural remedy used in China to improve strength and endurance. A small box sells for about three thousand dollars.

Pills containing a powder made from chopped-up and dried fetuses and newborn babies are smuggled into South Korea from China to allegedly boost sexual performance.

BABY BOOM

Each day there are 44,727 births in China and 26,106 deaths. Each day in India there are 76,517 births and 24,826 deaths.

A CUT ABOVE

Surat, India, is the world's largest diamond-cutting center.

It is estimated that Zimbabwe's government, led by President Robert Mugabe, has stolen at least $2 billion worth of diamonds from that country's mines.

CALL BEFORE DIGGING

In 2011, the country of Armenia lost its Internet service for twelve hours after a seventy-five-year-old woman severed the cable supplying service from Georgia with a shovel while scavenging for scrap metal.

MCDICK'S

There are numerous nicknames for McDonald's in various countries around the world. For example:

McDick's is used in Canada.

Macca's is used in Australia and New Zealand.

McDo is used in France.

McDoh is used in Quebec.

McDoof and Mekkes are used in Germany.

Makudo is used in Japan.

Mak Kee is used in Hong Kong.

Donken is used in Sweden.

Meki is used in Hungary.

Mec is used in Romania.

NO-NO NAMES

In Germany, names must indicate the sex of a child. In Iceland, if a name is not already on the National Register of Persons, an application must be reviewed by a federal committee to decide the name's suitability. New Zealand has a list of banned names.

MACHO MEN

Mustache implants are the hot new surgery for men in the Middle East, where thick, bushy 'staches are a symbol of male power and virility. The procedure involves transplanting hair from another part of the body and costs about seven thousand dollars.

MIND YOUR MANNERS

In southern China, flipping a whole fish over while eating it is considered bad luck.

Chileans don't eat anything with the fingers, not even French fries or pizza.

Italians don't drink cappuccino after 3 p.m.

The British always pass the port to the left.

When toasting someone in Germany, it is expected that you look the person directly in the eyes. To not do so is considered bad form, and superstition says both parties will be cursed to seven years of bad luck in the bedroom. Also, you should never ask for a refill before your entire glass is drained.

In France it is thought of poorly to pour oneself a refill without first offering the rest of the party one.

In Latin America it is considered bad luck to pour a drink with the left hand.

In Korea, women can only pour men's drinks, not other women's.

In China, France, Japan, and Saudi Arabia it is considered rude to blow one's nose in public. The Chinese and the Japanese also find the idea of handkerchiefs to be repellent.

NO-MAN'S-LAND

According to the Madrid Protocol of 1991, no country can own Antarctica and no mining, drilling for oil, hotels or resorts are allowed.

MONEY DOESN'T BUY EVERYTHING

In 2003, Mikhail Khodorkovsky, Russia's richest man and a frequent critic of Russian president Vladimir Putin, was arrested on what many believe to be politically motivated charges and sent to a prison camp, where he still remains.

RELIGION ROUNDUP

Mexico has the world's second-largest Catholic population.

One percent of the population of Japan is Christian.

There are 2.2 billion Christians in the world and 1.6 billion Muslims.

In 1910, there were just 9 million Christians in sub-Saharan Africa. That number had shot up to 516 million by 2011.

The Coptic Orthodox Christian Church selects a new pope by having a blindfolded altar boy pick a name from three that are placed into a large glass container.

WAYS TO GO

Belarus is the only country in Europe that has the death penalty.

> Only twenty-one countries worldwide have capital punishment—Belarus, Botswana, China, Cuba, Egypt, India, Indonesia, Iran, Iraq, Japan, Malaysia, Mongolia, North Korea, Pakistan, Saudi Arabia, Singapore, South Korea, Taiwan, Tonga, the United States, and Vietnam.

Up until the nineteenth century, execution by elephants was used in parts of Asia, particularly in India. The beasts would crush or dismember the condemned in public displays that could be carried out swiftly or prolonged as a form of torture.

> Death by slow slicing was a form of execution/torture that was employed in China from 900 to 1905. It involved removing portions of the body with a knife over an extended period of time, sometimes several days.

ARE YOU LONESOME TONIGHT?

About 60 percent of young men in Japan don't have girl-friends and 36 percent of sixteen- to nineteen-year-old males report having no interest in sex.

LOONEY LAWS

Although prostitution is legal in Iceland, strippers are outlawed.

In Afghanistan, a woman who gets raped may be charged with adultery and sent to prison. In some cases, she is encouraged to marry her attacker to restore her "honor." The babies of raped women serve the prison sentence with their mothers.

In the United Kingdom it is illegal for water bottlers to state that water can help prevent dehydration. This non-sensical ruling was handed down by the European Union Department of Health. Violators are subject to two years in jail.

In 2011, Saudi Arabia passed a law making it legal for women to work in lingerie stores. Before this, only men could work in malls and stores, since women are not allowed to mingle with men in public. Embarrassed female shoppers, accompanied by their equally embarrassed male guardians, had to shop together for undergarments sold by male salesclerks.

Saudi Arabia is the only country where it is illegal for women to drive.

It is now illegal to eat or drink in public areas around some of Rome's significant historical tourist attractions. Violators are subject to a $645 fine.

LOONIE TOONS

Canada uses one-dollar and two-dollar coins, known as loonies and toonies. The loonie bears an image of a common loon (a Canadian bird) and the toonie has the image of a polar bear.

THE LONG AND SHORT OF IT

The world's tallest Lego tower was built in Oslo, Norway, in 2010. It stood 30.22 meters high.

The world's longest wedding train was 2,750 meters.

The Pima Air and Space Museum in Tucson, Arizona, built a forty-five-foot-long paper airplane. The eight-hundred-pound aircraft actually flew at a speed of ninety-eight miles per hour after being towed aloft by a helicopter.

An ancient species of snake that lived in South America 60 million years ago weighed 2,500 pounds and stretched forty-three feet.

The world's shortest man is one Chandra Bahadur Dangi of Nepal, who stands just twenty-two inches tall. The seventy-two-year-old has five brothers, all of whom are normal size.

CATTLE EXCHANGE

South African president Jacob Zuma has been married six times and, as of 2012, has four wives. He paid the family of his fifth wife ten cattle in exchange for her hand in marriage.

RHODES TO RICHES

Women were not eligible for Rhodes Scholarships until 1977.

The scholarship is named after its benefactor, Cecil Rhodes, a South African–born Englishman who founded the De Beers diamond company.

The country of Rhodesia was named for Rhodes.

NO THANK YOU, SIR

The following men have turned down knighthoods from the British government:

Author Roald Dahl (*Charlie and the Chocolate Factory*) turned down his in 1986.

Writer Aldous Huxley (*Brave New World*) turned his down in 1959.

Author C. S. Lewis (*The Chronicles of Narnia*) likewise declined.

Novelist Evelyn Waugh (*Brideshead Revisited*) is reported to have regretted turning down his knighthood.

Alfred Hitchcock said "Cut" to the queen's first offer.

ASTRONOMICAL NUMBER

In 2006, the phone number 666-6666 was auctioned off in Qatar for $3 million.

VALUABLE VINEGAR

The world's most expensive bottle of wine was a 1787 Château Lafite that sold for $160,000 in 1985. The Bordeaux, which is now undrinkable because of its age, once belonged to Thomas Jefferson.

STORMY SEAS

The Bay of Bengal gets the most deadly storms of any region in the world.

IN THE RAW

Nyotaimori, meaning "female body presentation" in Japanese, is the practice of eating sashimi or sushi off the body of a nude female. A woman who specializes in this form of service must bathe first and douse herself with cold water so as not to warm up the food too quickly. She must also be able to lie perfectly still for hours.

BIG LOVE

The Jurassic Museum of Asturias in Spain features two life-size skeletons of *T. rex* copulating.

YANKEE GO HOME

The following are the countries that U.S. State Department advised Americans not to travel to in 2011: Afghanistan, Algeria, Chad, Colombia, Sudan (Darfur region), the Democratic Republic of the Congo, Haiti, Iraq, Kenya, Mali, Mauritania, Mexico, Niger, Pakistan, Nigeria, the Philippines, Somalia, and Yemen.

SOUTH OF THE BORDER

Approximately one in ten Mexicans live and work abroad, sending large sums of money to family members back home. In 2011, Mexican expatriates sent roughly $2 billion a month to banks in Mexico from money earned in the United States.

Mexico has the fourteenth-largest economy in the world, and the average salary there is higher than in Brazil, India, and China.

Mexico's official name is the United Mexican States. The country adopted the name in 1824 to emulate its neighbor to the north.

The Mexican drug lord Joaquín "El Chapo" Guzmán made the *Forbes* 2012 list of the world's wealthiest people, with an estimated worth of $1 billion.

The richest criminal of all time was Mexican Amado Carrillo Fuentes, whose drug empire gave him a net worth of about $25 billion before his death in 1997 from medical complications during facial plastic surgery to alter his appearance. (The two doctors who performed the surgery were later found dead, encased in concrete inside metal drums.)

An estimated thirteen thousand people died due to Mexican drug violence in 2011.

Drug smugglers in Mexico now shoot cans of marijuana across the U.S.-Mexico border with cannons.

BUSTED

The French government ruled that thirty thousand women who received PIP breast implants were to have them removed at the government's request, due to the concern that they may cause a rare type of cancer and are prone to rupture. The implants, which are made from a material intended for mattresses, were never approved for use in the United States.

FILL 'ER UP!

As of the end of 2012, the price of a gallon of gas was almost ten dollars in Turkey and just eighteen cents in Venezuela.

The world uses 89 million barrels of oil a day.

BACK TO THE FUTURE

At midnight on Thursday, December 29, 2011, Samoa skipped ahead to Saturday the 31st, omitting Friday the 30th. The country did so by shifting west of the International Date Line, to move them in line with the time zones of their major trading partner nations.

MONSTER MUM

The biggest chrysanthemum ever grown in North America was called a Thousand Bloom and had 1,167 flowers on a single plant. The monster mum, grown at Longwood Gardens in Pennsylvania, was twelve feet high and nearly six feet wide.

The world record holder mum is one grown in Japan that had 2,220 blooms.

AIRPORT REPORT

The runway at the Gibraltar Airport, in Gibraltar, has a main road that runs right across it. There are several flights in and out of the airport each day, and the roadway must be closed to allow the planes to take off and land.

The airport in the Maldives is on an artificial island in the middle of the Indian Ocean.

Frommers.com rated the ten best and worst airport terminals as follows:

- The best were Hajj Terminal, Jeddah, Saudi Arabia (this terminal is only open six weeks a year, during the Hajj pilgrimage to Mecca); Leifur Eiríksson Air Terminal, Keflavík, Iceland; Incheon Airport, Seoul, South Korea; "Rock" Terminal, Wellington, New Zealand; JFK Airport Terminal 5 (JetBlue), New York; Changi International Airport Terminal 3, Changi, Singapore; and Menara Airport Terminal 4, Marrakesh, Morocco).

- The worst airports included at number one JFK Airport Terminal 3, New York; at number seven LaGuardia Airport Terminal 5, New York; at number eight Newark Liberty International Airport Terminal B, Newark, New Jersey; and at number two Midway Airport, Chicago.

- According to a 2012 report, the world's top ten safest airlines are, in order, Finnair, New Zealand Air,

Cathay Pacific, Emirates, Etihad Airways, EVA Air, TAP Portugal, Hainan Airlines, Virgin Australia, and British Airways. None of these carriers had lost a plane or had a fatality in the past thirty years.

- China Airways, TAM Air, Air India, Gol Transportes Aéreos, Korean Air, Saudia Airlines, Turkish Airlines, Thai Airways, South African Airways, and SkyWest Airlines were the least safe airlines.

CATCH A WAVE

In 2011, surfer Garrett McNamara rode the biggest wave ever—a ninety-foot monster off the coast of Portugal.

CASH FLOW

In the aftermath of the devastating tsunami that swamped Japan in 2011, more than $78 million worth of cash has been recovered across the nation's countryside, most of it swept from homes and people. Amazingly, the large majority of the money was turned in to authorities.

BLACK AND BLUE

In 2012, Burger King Japan introduced the Premium Kuro Burger. It has a black bun made with bamboo charcoal in the dough, and black ketchup made with squid ink. McDonald's sells white- and black-bunned burgers in China.

The South Korean executive mansion where the president lives is called the Blue House. It has a blue-tiled roof.

BECAUSE, YOU NEVER KNOW . . .

Lloyd's of London issues some unique insurance policies, including insurance against giving birth to multiples, being struck by a meteorite or an asteroid hitting the Earth, or being abducted by an alien. One insurance company actually issued a policy in case the insured immaculately conceived the second incarnation of Jesus Christ.

KID CHARLEMAGNE

Genealogists say that anyone with European descendants is distantly related to Charlemagne.

GATES OF HELL

In 1971, Soviet geologists drilled into a subterranean cavern. The cavern collapsed, leaving a 230-foot-diameter hole in the ground filled with natural gas. The scientists set it afire in hopes it would burn off in a couple of days. The huge hole is still a raging inferno today and is known locally as "The Door to Hell."

KILLING FIELDS

After Afghanistan, Colombia leads the world in the annual number of people killed by land mines. The Revolutionary Armed Forces of Colombia (FARC), leftist rebels who have been trying to overthrow the government for fifty years, are responsible. FARC raises a lot of coca plants and protects the plantations with land mines. When they move to new locations, they leave the mines behind.

COCOA KIDS

According to the U.S. government, there are seventy-seven countries around the world where citizens are subjected to forced labor.

An estimated one hundred thousand child slaves work in the cocoa fields of West Africa.

BAGEL HEADS

The newest wacky fashion fad to hit Tokyo involves injecting a saline solution into the forehead, causing a huge welt, then pressing the thumb into the center to form a depression. The result is a deformity that closely resembles a bagel implanted on the forehead. The effect goes away in about a day.

TREE OF KNOWLEDGE

The most isolated tree in the world used to be L'Arbre du Ténéré. This acacia was located in the Sahara, in northeast Niger, 250 miles from the nearest tree, until it was knocked down by a drunken Libyan truck driver in 1973. It was replaced by a metal replica.

The stoutest tree in the world is Árbol del Tule, a Montezuma cypress in Mexico with a trunk circumference of 119 feet and a diameter of 37.5 feet.

Five of the ten most massive trees on Earth, measured by volume, are found in the Giant Forest of Sequoia National Park in California.

The boab prison tree in Wyndham, Western Australia, is an enormous boab tree with a hollow trunk that police on patrol once used as a temporary holding cell for prisoners being transported. The cavity measures about one hundred square feet.

There is an Antarctic beech tree in Queensland, Australia, that is about twelve thousand years old. These trees used to cover Antarctica in its warmer days. They moved northward as the climate cooled.

Quebec's maple trees produce 70 to 80 percent of the world's maple syrup.

One-third of the world's lumber comes from tree farms.

HEAVY IS THE HEAD THAT WEARS THE CROWN

The Crown Jewels of England are comprised of 23,578 gems.

The Imperial State Crown has 2,868 diamonds, 273 pearls, 17 sapphires, 11 emeralds, and 5 rubies.

In 2011, the British monarchy changed its rules of succession. Now a firstborn daughter can ascend to the throne, even if she has a younger brother. Had this policy been in place five hundred years ago, Henry VIII would have lost out to his older sister Margaret, who would have become queen.

MURDER CENTRAL

The murder rate in Caracas, Venezuela, is higher than that of Baghdad.

CAPTAIN HOOK

A Dutch group of doctors called Women on Waves runs what is called an "abortion ship" that sails to countries where abortion is illegal, picks up women there, and takes them into international waters to perform the procedure, before returning them home.

MUMMY DEAREST

Sokushinbutsu was a practice where Japanese Buddhist monks mummified themselves. For one thousand days they would eat only nuts and seeds, while exercising strenuously to reduce body fat. For the next one thousand days, they would eat only bark and roots and would drink a poisonous tea made from a tree resin that's used as a lacquer. This resulted in vomiting, loss of fluids, and making the body too toxic for maggots to eat after death. Finally, the monks would assume the lotus position in a small stone tomb, until they died.

Hundreds of monks attempted self-mummification, but only a dozen or two have been found so far. Those who were found were removed from the tomb and displayed as a Buddha in their temple.

LE PEW

A 2012 poll found that one in five French citizens bathe every other day, and 3.5 percent do so only once a week. And 20 percent of the population admits to not washing their hands before meals, and 12 percent fail to do so after using the bathroom.

COKELESS COUNTRY

About 80 percent of Cuba's labor force work for the government.

Coca-Cola is sold in every country except Cuba and North Korea.

DEEP THOUGHTS

Nemo 3 is the deepest recreational pool in the world. Located in Brussels, Belgium, the 113-foot-deep swimming pool is used for indoor diving. It holds 2.5 million liters of water.

The underground Sifto Salt Mine in Ontario, Canada, is larger in area than Manhattan.

STREET SKINNY

The world's narrowest street is Spreuerhofstrasse in Reutlingen, Germany, which is thirty centimeters at its narrowest and fifty centimeters at its widest.

BLOCKBUSTER BREW

The world's strongest beer is Scotland's Brewmeister's Armageddon, which has an alcohol content by volume of 65 percent. That's 130 proof.

IT'S ALL DEPENDS

In Japan, the sales of adult diapers exceed those of baby diapers.

WAY BACK WHEN

THIS OLD HOUSE

The oldest wooden building in North America is Fairbanks House outside of Boston, which was occupied by the Fairebankes family for eight generations. The house, which was built circa 1640, is now a museum.

> The oldest church in America is San Miguel Mission in Santa Fe, New Mexico, which was built in 1710. Masses are still held there.

Lafitte's Blacksmith Shop Bar on Bourbon Street in New Orleans is the oldest operating tavern in the United States. It first opened circa 1722 and later served as a hangout for notorious pirates Jean and Pierre Lafitte.

HAWAII FAUX-O

Tiki bars were first introduced to the world in the 1930s by two California restaurants—Trader Vic's and Don the Beachcomber. (A tiki is a carved figure of the Maori people of New Zealand.)

Grass skirts are from the Gilbert Islands in the Pacific. They were introduced to Hawaii in the 1870s. Before this, Hawaiians wore skirts made of fresh ti leaves.

BACK IN BLACK

Prior to 1913, Ford automobiles came in many colors, but not black. Then, in 1914, as a cost-cutting measure, black was the only color offered.

NAME THAT CAR

Originally, the Volkswagen Beetle was named *Kraft durch Freude Wagen*, or the "Strength Through Joy Car," at Adolf Hitler's behest.

Some other interesting car names of the past include the Mazda Bongo Friendee, which was made from 1995 to 2005; the Honda That's, sold from 2002 to 2007; and the Studebaker Dictator, available from 1927 to 1937.

HISTORY UNCOVERED

The earliest known bras were found in an Austrian castle and date to the Middle Ages. The bra was previously thought to have been invented in the early 1900s. This find pushes that date back some five hundred years.

Panty hose were invented in the 1950s.

The sales of panty hose did not exceed those of stockings until 1970.

Sales of panty hose went down 50 percent between 1995 and 2006.

STERILIZED STATES

Between 1909 and 1963, the state of California sterilized 20,000 people who were wards of the state. Virginia sterilized 8,300. In total, thirty-two states engaged in eugenics.

The Nazis consulted with the state of California before setting up their own eugenics program.

THE TIMES THEY ARE A CHANGIN'

A century ago, there were 230,000 blacksmiths in the United States. Today there are just 600.

Western Union sent its last telegram in 2006.

Old lifejackets were filled with cork.

Early slot machine prizes were a cigar and a drink.

WORLD AT WAR

Marquis de Lafayette was a nineteen-year-old French aristocrat who financed his own way to America to fight in the Revolutionary War. He had to purchase his own ship and disguise himself as a woman to leave Europe. Congress rewarded Lafayette by giving the teenager the rank of major general.

No American forces were killed when George Washington captured Trenton on December 26, 1776. The Hessian commander of the garrison received a letter from a Loyalist warning him of the sneak attack just before it happened, but he was too busy playing cards to read it.

There is a cemetery in Tripoli, Libya, that has the remains of thirteen U.S. sailors who died there in 1804 when the USS *Intrepid* blew up on a secret mission in the First Barbary War.

American naval captain James Lawrence uttered the famous words "Don't give up the ship" after being mortally wounded aboard the U.S. ship *Chesapeake* during the War of 1812. Unfortunately, the British did capture the ship shortly thereafter.

More British Redcoats were killed by the tornado and storm that hit Washington, DC, during their occupation of that city in the War of 1812 than were killed by American forces.

The biggest foreign invasion onto U.S. soil occurred in 1814, when the British lost to American forces in the Battle of Plattsburgh at Lake Champlain, New York.

In 1814, President Andrew Jackson pardoned notorious pirate Jean Lafitte and his men in exchange for their help in defeating the British at the Battle of New Orleans. After the battle, Lafitte returned to his pirating ways.

> During the Russian Campaign of 1812, Napoléon lost two hundred thousand horses.

Napoléon Bonaparte, at five feet seven inches, was not short when compared to the height of most Frenchmen of his time.

> The convention of the time during the Civil War was for women to mourn six months for the death of a brother, one year for the death of a child, and two and a half years for the death of a husband. They went through three stages of mourning—heavy, full, and half—with gradually decreasing requirements for dress and behavior. Men, on the other hand, were only expected to mourn for three months for the death of a wife and to wear a black band on the arm or hat.

After the Battle of Shiloh, the wounds of some of the casualties glowed in the dark. Many wounded lay in the mud for two days and got hypothermic. Their lowered body temperature encouraged the growth of the bioluminescent bacterium *Photorhabdus luminescens*. Those with the glowing wounds healed faster, as the bacterium inhibited the growth of pathogens in the wounds.

During the Civil War there was a Union general named Jefferson Davis, also the name of the president of the Confederacy.

A five-dollar Confederate bill featuring Jefferson Davis was found in the wallet of Abraham Lincoln after he was assassinated.

The worst civilian disaster during the Civil War occurred on September 17, 1862, at the Allegheny Arsenal in Lawrenceville, Pennsylvania. Seventy-eight women and children employed to stuff, roll, and tie ammunition during the Battle of Antietam were killed when a wagonload of gunpowder being delivered from DuPont exploded because of sparks from the horses' iron horseshoes on new stone. This explosion triggered two more blasts. It is believed that leaky barrels used by DuPont and road stones that were too hard caused the disaster.

Sergeant Stubby was America's first war dog. He achieved the rank of sergeant for his valor in combat during World War I. He was able to smell poison gas before the other soldiers and hear incoming artillery before them also. He single-pawedly captured a German spy. Upon his return home Stubby became a national hero and a celebrity and met three different U.S presidents.

In 1940, the Soviet secret police massacred twenty-two thousand Polish military officers in the Katyn Forest. The United States knew about it but kept quiet for fear of upsetting Josef Stalin, who would later be an American ally when the United States entered the war.

At the peak of World War II, the U.S. Navy had 1,248 active ships in its fleet. By 2011, that number was down to 285.

The last U.S. cavalry charge came in 1942, on the island of Luzon in the Philippines.

In 1939, in the biggest financial transaction in world history, Britain shipped $7 billion worth of its gold reserves, stocks, and bonds to Canada aboard a light frigate to protect these assets from the Nazis. England's National Gallery moved countless priceless works of art to tunnels at a quarry in North Wales. The hiding place of the Crown Jewels still hasn't been revealed to this day.

Yonatan Netanyahu, the older brother of Israeli prime minister Benjamin Netanyahu, was the commander of the elite Israeli commando unit that rescued more than one hundred hostages on a plane that was hijacked and flown to Entebbe Airport in Uganda in 1976. He was the only one of the commandos who was killed.

The Iran-Iraq War (1980–88) is the only military conflict in which helicopters engaged each other in aerial combat.

All the germ strains used by Iraq to develop its biological warfare weapons program came from the United States. They were supplied by the Centers for Disease Control and Prevention (CDC) and the American Type Culture Collection (a biological sample company) in the 1980s. The CDC claims it thought the anthrax, botulinum toxin, and West Nile virus would be used for medical research.

Navy SEAL sniper Chris Kyle holds the record for most confirmed kills in U.S. military history—160. Kyle served ten years in Iraq and was so feared by the Iraqis that they nicknamed him the "Devil of Ramadi" and placed an eighty-thousand-dollar bounty on his head. Ironically, Kyle did not die in combat, but was murdered on a Texas gun range in 2013 by a fellow veteran suffering from post-traumatic stress disorder.

The world's current longest-running war is the civil war in Myanmar that pits the Karen people against the central government. It has been raging since 1949.

Florence Green, the last known veteran of World War I, died in London in 2012. She served in the Women's Royal Air Force.

THE RIGHT STUFF

Seventy-four graduates from the U.S. Military Academy at West Point have won the Medal of Honor.

Eighteen West Point grads went on to become as-tronauts, as did thirty-nine from the U.S. Air Force Academy and more than fifty from the U.S. Naval Academy.

MAN WHO SAVED THE WORLD

During the Cuban Missile Crisis in 1962, the Soviets sent a flotilla of nuclear-armed submarines to the waters near the United States. Soviet submarine B-59 had been out of contact with Moscow for several days and had no idea what the status of the crisis was. When the U.S. Navy dropped depth charges to signal B-59 to surface, its cap-tain thought that a war had begun. He and the chief polit-ical officer on board wanted to launch a nuclear torpedo at the Americans, which would have likely started World War III and led to Armageddon. Protocol dictated that use of a nuke would require the approval of these two men as well as that of second-in-command Vasili Arkhipov, who defied the others and refused to consent.

The only American killed by enemy fire during the Cuban Missile Crisis was U2 spy plane pilot Rudolph Anderson, who was shot down over Cuba during a reconnaissance flight.

DO NOT ENTER

In 1939, the luxury liner *Hamburg American* brought 936 Jewish refugees from Germany to Cuba. Upon their arrival, the passengers were told that they had been duped out of their money and would not be allowed into the country. The ship then sailed to Miami, where the U.S. government also denied them entry. Eventually, England, Holland, Belgium, and France took the Jews. Unfortunately, the latter three nations were later overrun by the Nazis and many of the Jews became victims of the Holocaust.

> During World War II, many Jewish refugees in Russia ended up in Japan, the only country that would take them.

During World War II, black American troops were banned from Australia and Iceland.

FENCE SITTERS

Ireland remained neutral in World War II and refused to allow Britain the use of its ports and airfields.

> The Irish prime minister expressed his condolences to Germany upon Hitler's death.

The neutral country of Portugal flew its flags at half staff to mourn Hitler's passing.

PATTON PLACE

During World War II, American general George Patton stopped halfway across the Rhine to urinate in the river. He liked to mark his territory, much as predatory animals do.

Patton's great uncle was a Confederate colonel killed during Pickett's Charge at the Battle of Gettysburg.

When Patton was sent south of the border into Mexico during the Punitive Expedition of 1916, he returned to the United States with two dead Mexican leaders strapped to his armored vehicle, like big game killed in the hunt, making him a sensation in the press.

Patton believed that he was the reincarnation of the ancient military leader Hannibal.

TAKING ONE FOR THE TEAM

Civil War political figure and lawyer Clement Vallandigham accidentally killed himself while defending a client against a murder charge in 1871. His client was accused of shooting a man in a barroom brawl, but Vallandigham argued that the victim had shot himself while trying to pull a gun out of his shirt. When Vallandigham attempted to recreate the shooting, he shot himself in the process, with a gun he believed to be empty. His point proved, the client was found not guilty.

LONDON FOG

One reason London was so foggy in the old days was due to air pollution, or smog. The famed London "fog" is now a thing of the past.

In Victorian London the mail was delivered seven times a day.

The reason London police are known as "bobbies" is because the Metropolitan Police Force was founded by an act of Parliament introduced by Sir Robert (Bobbie) Peel in 1829.

The Crystal Palace, built in London for the Great Exposition of 1851, had the world's first public toilets, known as the "Retiring Rooms." 827,280 people each spent a penny to use the facilities. Using the lavatory is still referred to as "spending a penny" in England.

CLOTHESHORSE

The Aztec ruler, Montezuma, was quite the clotheshorse. He wore four different outfits each day and never the same one twice.

OGRE'S OFFSPRING

Josef Stalin's daughter, Svetlana, defected from the Soviet Union in 1967, while in India, leaving her children behind. Her notorious father had died in 1953.

Svetlana was the darling of the Soviet Union as a child, with countless baby girls named after her.

Svetlana's mother committed suicide when she was six.

Her brother, Yakov, shot himself in the head because of his father's brutality toward him, but survived. Stalin remarked afterward that his son "can't even shoot straight." During World War II, Yakov was captured by the Germans. They offered to swap him for a captured German field marshal held by the Soviets, but Stalin refused. Yakov then succeeded in killing himself while in a POW camp.

HOLY UNACCEPTABLE

Pope John XXIII, who ruled from 1410 to 1415, was an ex-pirate. His campaign to become pope was funded by the powerful Medici family. Once in power, John XXIII made the Medici Bank the official bank of the papacy.

John XXIII was defrocked for corruption and fornication.

Pope Leo X had an elaborate celebration when he was elected pope in 1513. He had a young boy painted entirely gold for the gala. The unfortunate child died soon afterward.

A pope who is considered an illegal claimant of the Holy See is known as an antipope. Such popes sit in opposition to a legally elected or sitting pope and sometimes enjoy more widespread support than the actual pope. There have been about forty antipopes.

Between 1409 and 1413, there were three different men who simultaneously claimed to be pope, one in Avignon (in France), one in Pisa, and one in Rome.

CHRIST-CROSS

Early Christians began the practice of crossing fingers as a symbol of the cross. They did so secretly to recognize one another during the time of the Roman persecution and to help ward off evil.

ABOUT FACE

Muslims used to pray facing Jerusalem, not Mecca.

TILL DEATH DO US PART

During the Middle Ages, in Germanic countries, two parties could settle a dispute in the absence of any witnesses or evidence by engaging in a judicial duel. These fights to the death were overseen by a judge/justice, and the survivor was deemed to be right in the eyes of the law.

Men and women, sometimes a husband and wife, could engage each other in a judicial duel. To make for a fairer fight, the man had to stand in a hole up to his waist and was given a pointy wooden club to fight with, while the woman could move freely and fought with a large rock wrapped in the end of her veil, which she would swing at her spouse.

COLA WARS

In the early 1930s, the owner of Pepsi offered to sell his company to the Coca-Cola Company, but they weren't interested.

By the mid-1980s, Pepsi had a bigger market share than Coke.

In 1985, Coca-Cola was reformulated as New Coke to make it sweeter and less acidic—like Pepsi. New Coke replaced Coke on April 23, 1985. Public outcry forced the company to bring Coke back, as Coca-Cola Classic, on July 10 of the same year.

CONTRARY TO POPULAR BELIEF

A vomitorium was not a place where Romans would puke after a meal to make room for more food. Such a custom was never practiced. A vomitorium was actually a passageway beneath a stadium that allowed rapid flow of spectators in and out. The word derives from the Latin verb *vomeo*, meaning "to spew forth."

Nero did not fiddle while Rome burned, but immediately became involved in relief efforts to feed and house the victims.

The Vikings did not wear horns on their helmets. This misconception probably began with an 1876 production of the Richard Wagner opera *Der Ring des Nibelungen.*

The Pilgrims did not necessarily wear all black, but rather they also wore a variety of colors.

The first American Thanksgiving was not celebrated by the Pilgrims in Plymouth in 1621. Several others predate this, including ones in St. Augustine, Florida, in 1565; Jamestown, Virginia, in 1607; and the Berkeley Hundred in the Virginia Colony in 1619. The myth of the Pilgrims being first was promoted by nineteenth-century writer Sarah Josepha Hale, who was pushing for a national day of Thanksgiving.

The Emancipation Proclamation did not abolish slavery in the United States. It only applied to states that had seceded from the Union, who ignored it. The Union's slaveholding border states of Delaware, Maryland, Kentucky, Missouri, and West Virginia were exempt. Slavery was not abolished until the Thirteenth Amendment was passed in 1865.

The story of Mrs. O'Leary's cow starting the Great Chicago Fire of 1871 was made up by a newspaper reporter looking for a good story.

Albert Einstein never failed a math class and had mastered calculus by age fifteen.

THE REAL MCCOYS

The Hatfields were from West Virginia and the McCoys from Kentucky. The two clans were separated by the Tug Fork River.

The feud between the two families resulted in twelve deaths between 1880 and 1891.

The U.S. Supreme Court became involved in the feud after a Kentucky posse captured eight Hatfields and brought them across state lines for trial.

In 1888, the eight Hatfields were tried and convicted for having killed one of the McCoys. Seven got life sentences and another was hanged. This essentially put an end to the feud.

In 1979, members of each family reunited on the TV game show *Family Feud*. One of the prizes was a pig that was kept on stage for the run of the weeklong series of shows. (Ownership of a pig was one of the root causes of the feud.)

THAT'S A LOTTO MONEY

Legend has it that writer/philosopher Voltaire and a friend noticed that the prize in the French lottery in 1728 was much bigger than the cost of all the tickets being sold. They formed a syndicate and bought up all the tickets, winning a large sum of money.

IT TAKES TWO

The tango was considered an obscene lower-class dance, until it migrated to Europe in the early twentieth century and was embraced by Parisian high society.

FAR-OFF FRIENDS

In 1777, Morocco became the first foreign country to recognize America as a unified sovereign nation.

THAT BITES

Alexander I of Greece died in 1920, after a macaque on the palace grounds bit him and the wound became infected.

WELCOME TO THE PARTY

The Republican Party began as an antislavery third party and quickly became a force in the 1856 and 1860 elections. Before this, the Democrats and the Whigs were the main parties.

Not Necessarily the News

MON DIEU!

In 2012, a 140,000-square-foot French château was bull-dozed to the ground by mistake. The construction company was supposed to raze a smaller structure on the property and refurbish the mansion. Somehow they got confused.

ARE WE THERE YET?

In December 2012, a 125-mile-long traffic jam on Russia's M-10 highway stretched from St. Petersburg to Moscow. Fog and heavy snow were to blame.

HO, HO, OH NO!

In 2011, an eighteen-year-old California man got stuck in the chimney of his family's home while trying to sneak in after his curfew. He was found with his feet hanging in the fireplace. Firefighters pulled the Santa wannabe back up and out using ropes and a ladder.

PISS DRUNK

In 2012, a Colorado woman was arrested after punching a $30 million Clyfford Still oil painting and then pulling down her pants and urinating on it. The drunken art critic, Carmen Tisch, caused $10,000 worth of damage to the picture hanging in a Denver museum.

HIGHWAY TO HELL

In 2012, a New Hampshire women, one Joyce Coffey, was arrested four times in twenty-six hours—three times for playing the AC/DC song "Highway to Hell" too loudly and once for throwing a frying pan at her nephew.

BUSTED

In 2012, a Panamanian woman was arrested at a Barcelona, Spain, airport after coming in on a flight from Bogotá, Colombia, when security agents noticed that she had bloody bandages under her breasts. She was taken to a hospital, where doctors removed two breast implants that were packed with three pounds of cocaine.

FATAL PHONE

In 2012, a Ugandan man contracted the deadly Ebola virus after stealing a cell phone from a patient quarantined at a hospital. The man subsequently was admitted to the same hospital for treatment.

WHIZ KIDS

American Taylor Wilson became the youngest person to build a nuclear fusion reactor, at age fourteen, in 2008.

Six-year-old Lori Anne Madison of Virginia in 2012 became the youngest person ever to qualify for the National Spelling Bee.

FLOTSAM FLOTILLA

In 2012, a huge mass of pumice, eight times the area of Rhode Island, was found floating in the South Pacific. (Pumice is a lightweight volcanic stone that floats in water and is commonly used to smooth skin.)

WHERE'S WILSON?

Sixty-seven-year-old Jennifer Wilson of England spent much of her life searching for her twin sister from whom she was separated at birth. In 2010, a TV production company, doing a show on reuniting families, finally found her sister, who had always lived just three miles away and had the same dentist and doctor.

IN YOUR HONOR

Former Arapahoe County, Colorado, sheriff Patrick Sullivan Jr. was arrested in 2011 on charges that he traded drugs for sex with other men. The former national "Sheriff of the Year," ironically, was sent to the Patrick

J. Sullivan Jr. Detention Facility, which is named in his honor.

ADDING INSULT TO INJURY

In 2011, a Kansas couple was held captive in their home by criminal Jesse Dimmick, who was on the run from the police. Dimmick, who had a knife, offered the couple an unspecified amount of money if they wouldn't call the authorities. When Dimmick fell asleep, they did so. Dimmick, who is serving an eleven-year sentence for the kidnapping, sued the couple for breach of oral contract and is seeking damages for the $235,000 medical bill he incurred after police shot him while they were rescuing the couple.

NO HORSING AROUND

In 2011, Congress removed restrictions on the sale of horsemeat for human consumption in the United States.

DYING TO MAKE A POINT

In 1993, Toronto lawyer Garry Hoy died while demonstrating to a group of his partners that windows on the twenty-fourth floor of the Toronto-Dominion Centre were unbreakable. Hoy threw himself against a window. It didn't break, but popped out of its frame, falling twenty-four floors to the ground, along with Hoy.

EASY COME, EASY GO

In 2011, a Utah man wrecked a $380,000 Lamborghini Murciélago roadster he had won in a convenience store contest, a mere six hours after picking it up.

CHUBSY-UBSY

In 2011, there was a three-year-old boy in China who weighed 132 pounds. He had weighed just 5.7 pounds at birth.

THAT'S USING YOUR HEAD

In July 2011, a motorcyclist in Onondaga, New York, riding without a helmet to protest the state's helmet law, died when he flipped over the handlebars and landed on his head on the pavement. Police said he probably would have lived if he had been wearing a helmet.

FLIGHTS OF FRIGHT

On a 2011 Comtel Air flight from India to England, the plane landed in Vienna and the crew demanded hundreds of dollars from each passenger for fuel if they wished to continue on to their destination. Airline officials said later that none of the cash was given to the company.

In 2012, a British Airways flight from Miami to London announced while over the Atlantic Ocean that the plane was about to make a water landing. The warning was repeated again before the crew calmed the passengers down and told them the announcement had been made in error.

In 2011, a pilot in a holding pattern around New York's LaGuardia Airport stepped out of the cabin for a moment to use the restroom. He somehow got locked inside and could not get out. He pounded on the door to alert passengers. A man with a thick accent knocked on the cockpit door to tell the copilot, but spooked him instead. Thinking terrorists were taking over the plane, the copilot radioed for help. Fighter jets were alerted and the FBI met the plane upon landing.

In 2012, the TSA at Las Vegas McCarran Airport refused to allow a woman on a plane because there was gel-like frosting on a cupcake she had in her carry-on bag.

In 2011, model Lauren Scruggs was severely injured when she accidentally walked into the still-spinning propeller of the small plane she had just flown in. Scruggs lost her left hand and eye and had extensive facial damage.

In 2010, a teen snuck into the wheel well of a plane waiting to take off from Charlotte Douglas International Airport and bound for Boston. He plummeted to his death when the landing gear was lowered outside of Boston before landing. Naturally, his parents have sued the airline.

Also in 2010, a small plane in the Democratic Republic of the Congo crashed, killing twenty passengers, after a crocodile smuggled on board got loose and caused everyone to rush to the front of the craft in a panic and the pilot to lose control. One passenger and said crocodile survived.

In 2006, an unnamed airline mechanic was sucked into the engine of a jetliner at El Paso International Airport, with predictable results.

NO TANKS!

In 2004, the city council of Monza, Italy, outlawed the keeping of goldfish in curved bowls since the bent light would give them a distorted view of the outside world.

GUEST SERVICES

Vanisha Mittal, daughter of a billionaire steel magnate, married investment banker Amit Bhatia in 2005. The $60 million wedding featured invitations mailed in silver boxes, plane fare, accommodations at five-star hotels in Paris and Versailles, and gift bags filled with jewels for the guests. Kylie Minogue performed at the reception.

STICKUPS

In 2008, in broad daylight, the Harry Winston jewelry store in Paris was robbed of jewels with a retail value of $110 million. One year earlier, the same store had been robbed of 10 million euros worth of jewels.

In 2011, a modern-day Robin Hood was arrested shortly after holding up a Boston bank and then being found handing out cash to children in a park.

BETTER LUCK NEXT TIME

In 2012, a man apparently trying to kill himself went over Niagara Falls and survived the 180-foot drop, swimming to shore afterward.

Ponzi schemer Bernie Madoff and his wife both attempted suicide by taking overdoses of prescription sleeping pills on the Christmas Eve after his crimes were exposed. While both survived, the Madoffs' son, Mark, hung himself in December 2010.

RAILROADED

A Chicago court ruled that a man who was killed by a train while crossing the tracks at a station could be held liable after part of his body flew into and injured a by-stander. In 2008, an unspecified part of Hiroyuki Joho's body was flung into Gayane Zokhrabov. She sued Joho's estate for damages and won. The court found that "it was reasonably foreseeable" that the train would hit Joho and hurl his body toward the platform.

In 2012, two different men were killed on opposite sides of the state of Florida (435 miles away) by the same train on the same day.

NICE TRY

In 2011, one Michael Fuller was arrested at a North Carolina Walmart after trying to pay for his purchase with a $1 million bill. He insisted it was real and refused to leave until police arrived on the scene.

GET STUFFED

In 2011, six-hundred-pound Donna Simpson, holder of the Guinness World Record for the "World's Heaviest Mother," shut down her "feederism" website and decided to promote healthy eating. "Feederish" is a type of fetish where people get excitement by watching extremely fat women eat. Simpson pulled in ninety thousand dollars a year from subscribers who would pay to view her stuff herself with various foods, while trying to pack on as many pounds as possible. Some men would even send her additional money and a grocery shopping list with foods they wanted to see her eat.

Twenty-one-year-old Kerry Trebilcock of England has eaten more than four thousand sponges and one hundred pounds of organic soap since being infected with hookworm in 2008. She enjoys the sponges with BBQ sauce or ketchup.

BIGGEST LOSER

Englishman Paul Mason used to be billed as the "world's fattest man." By the end of 2012, he had shed 650 pounds after a gastric bypass procedure and diet modification. Before this, he weighed 1,000 pounds and ate twenty thousand calories a day, including up to forty bags of potato chips.

BOOZE NEWS

The American Automobile Association (AAA) has instituted a "Tipsy Tow" program, where members too drunk to drive themselves home can call and get their car towed home and a ride with the driver. The program is offered in select areas on certain days, such as Thanksgiving, New Year's Eve, Memorial Day, the Fourth of July, and Super Bowl Sunday.

DR. NO!!

In 2011, a woman in Florida, who aspired to work in a nightclub, went to a person she believed to be a doctor to have her buttocks enhanced. Oneal Ron Morris, a man posing as a woman and claiming to be an MD, injected the woman's behind repeatedly with a mixture of cement, flat tire sealant, and mineral oil for the sum of seven hundred dollars. Predictably, the woman ended up hospitalized.

In 2012, a fake doctor in San Francisco performed liposuction on a woman while smoking a cigar and making her hold her IV bag during the procedure. The woman, who thought she was getting a real bargain, came to regret her choice of "physicians" after the inevitable complications developed.

Among the bizarre items found in people's rectums at emergency rooms in 2011 were a Buzz Lightyear doll, a Barbie, a large kitchen knife, and a revolver. The explanations of how these things got there were often as bizarre as the items themselves.

Like a scene from a bad movie, Pennsylvanian Ed Juchniewicz died in 1991 after the unattended ambulance stretcher he was strapped to rolled down a hill and turned over.

In 2001, six-year-old New Yorker Michael Colombini was killed during an MRI procedure. A portable oxygen tank was brought near the machine's magnetic field and flew into the boy's head.

In 2010, a U.S. military veteran's penis got frostbitten in a VA medical center and required amputation after nurses left an ice pack on his member for nineteen straight hours following a surgical procedure down there.

In 1974, British health food advocate Basil Brown died after drinking too much carrot juice.

ONE WEDDING AND A FUNERAL

In 2012, a Thai man married his girlfriend of ten years after she died, in a combination wedding/funeral ceremony. She was buried in her wedding dress.

PIGGING OUT

In 2012, an Oregon farmer, Terry Vance Garner, was eaten by his pigs, some of which weighed seven hundred pounds. All that remained was the man's dentures and a few body parts.

BIG MAC ATTACK

In 2012, a North Carolina woman who didn't feel like waiting in line at the local McDonald's drive-thru, bypassed the order speaker, cut in line to the pickup window, and tried to place her order there. When employees denied her service, she refused to leave and the police were summoned after twenty minutes. She was Tasered after resisting arrest, and her two-year-old daughter was taken into protective custody.

FISHY FINGERS

In July 2012, a man lost four of his fingers while wakeboarding on a lake in Idaho. Two months later, a fisherman on the same lake caught a trout that had one of the man's fingers in its belly.

SHOCK AND AWE

An iPhone 4 survived a fall of 13,500 feet when it came out of the pocket of its skydiving owner. The screen shattered, but the phone still worked.

HIS DAYS WERE NUMBERED

Dominic Calgi's New York license plate number—5V 17 32—matched the date of his death—May 17, 1932.

CASHIN' IN

A rare copy of the first Superman comic book sold for $1 million in 2010.

In 2011, a tintype photograph of Billy the Kid, the only known image of him, sold for $2.3 million.

In recent years, several paintings by American artist Martin Johnson Heade were accidentally discovered by lucky people. Two works were purchased for $60 at an estate auction in Arizona in 1996 and sold for over $1 million. Another was bought for $29 at a Wisconsin rummage sale in 1999 and sold at auction for $882,500. In 2003, a Heade was found in an attic outside Boston and auctioned off for more than $1 million. A Florida woman's son had her get an appraisal on a little painting hanging in her living room, purchased for a few dollars years earlier, after seeing a Heade work on TV. It sold at auction for $218,500 in 2004.

The world's oldest still-running automobile is an 1884 steam-powered De Dion Bouton et Trépardoux Dos-a-Dos Steam Runabout that sold for $4.62 million in 2011.

A Peugeot once owned by Iranian president Mahmoud Ahmadinejad sold for $2.4 million.

VIRGIN AIRWAYS

In 2012, twenty-year-old Brazilian Catarina Migliorini auctioned off her virginity for the documentary *Virgin Wanted*. The anonymous winning bidder came up with $780,000 and will deflower the young lady aboard a flight from Australia to the United States to avoid prostitution charges.

FOR WHOM THE BELL TOLLS

As of 2012, a New Jersey scofflaw has racked up over $120,000 in fines for blowing through various tolls over the years to buy drugs in New York. Worse yet, Peter Davis used his mother Jean's car and now she is on the hook for the money and is reported on the Port Authority of New York and New Jersey website as owing the most of any scofflaw.

THE WORLD'S BREAST ICE CREAM

In 2011, a London ice cream shop—Icecreamists—sold "Baby Gaga," an ice cream made from human breast milk blended with vanilla bean pods and lemon zest. It sold for $22.50 a serving, until local health authorities put an end to it.

BURN NOTICE

In 2012, the maker of Banana Boat sunscreen recalled five hundred thousand bottles of its spray-on lotion because several people caught on fire after applying the product and getting too close to an open flame.

ODDS ARE

In 2009, the same six winning numbers (4, 15, 23, 24, 35, and 42) came up in two consecutive drawings of the lottery in Bulgaria. Eighteen Bulgarians profited by playing the six numbers on the second drawing, after no one won the time before.

Also in 2009, the numbers 4-1-9 came up in consecutive Pick 3 drawings in Michigan and the numbers 3-7-5 came up in two consecutive New York drawings.

In 2000, a Washington State newspaper accidentally printed the Pick 4 winning numbers for the Oregon lottery the day *before* the drawing. They did this by mistakenly publishing the prior day's winning Virginia numbers (6-8-5-5) for the previous day's winning Oregon numbers, which happened to be the next day's winning Oregon numbers.

BATHROOM BLAST

In 2012, more than 2 million Flushmate III pressure-assisted flushing systems, a water conservation device installed in toilet tanks, were recalled because they might explode. Some 304 reports of exploding toilets, many resulting in severe lacerations and impact injuries, prompted the action.

KIDS DO THE DARNEDEST THINGS

A boy in the Ukraine found his parents' savings hidden in the couch and spent nearly four thousand dollars on candy over the course of several days in 2012.

> In 2011, a thirteen-year-old Albuquerque, New Mexico, student was arrested, handcuffed, and hauled away by police for burping in gym class.

In 2012, a Pennsylvania boy destroyed thirty-six thousand dollars' worth of computers in his elementary school by urinating on them.

> The National Transportation Safety Board found that a fatal 2010 helicopter plane crash in Phoenix, Arizona, was caused when the billionaire owner of the craft let his five-year-old daughter sit on his lap while he was in the copilot's seat and she kicked the flight controls, sending five people to their deaths.

KILLER KITTY

In a fifteen-month stretch of time from 2011 through 2012, a large man-eating leopard devoured fifteen different people in Nepal.

BAZOOKA GUM

In 2009, Ukrainian chemistry student Vladimir Likho-nos accidentally put a piece of gum he was chewing in an explosive mixture he was working on. When he resumed chewing, he blew off his jaw and lower face.

EVERY VOTE COUNTS

After the 2012 presidential election, an Arizona woman ran over her husband with her car because he didn't vote.

TILL DEATH DO US PART

In 2012, a Kansas couple who had been married for sixty-two years died within hours of each other. Just after Melvin Cornelson succumbed to cancer, his wife Doris, who had remained at his side, went off to bed and never woke up.

PREMATURE IGNITION

In 1960, more than one hundred Soviet scientists and offi-cials were burned to a crisp when the rocket booster engine they were preparing for launch suddenly ignited after a switch was accidentally turned on.

WORDSMITH

Originally, the word *pea* came into the English language as "pease," for the singular form (as in pease pudding) and "peasen" for the plural.

The word *autumn* for the season between summer and winter began to gradually replace the word "harvest" in English in the fourteenth century. By the seventeenth century, "harvest" was gone and the word "fall" came into usage. Since the nineteenth century, the word "autumn" has been predominate, while "autumn" and "fall" are used interchangeably in the United States.

Pit stop refers to the practice of servicing autos in the days before lifts, which involved working from a pit beneath the car.

The *dumb blonde* stereotype probably arose from a famed blond sixteenth-century French courtesan named Rosalie Duthe, who was known for hesitating a long time while speaking, making her appear dim-witted and mute (dumb). She was satirized in a 1775 play.

Can't hold a candle to comes from the days when an apprentice would hold a candle so the more experienced craftsman could see what he was doing. The candleholder was thus the inferior.

Don't look a gift horse in the mouth has to do with the buying of a horse, where it was common practice to inspect its teeth to see how old it was. This practice also is the origin of the phrase *long in the tooth*.

A *blockbuster* was a very powerful bomb used during World War II. The word has since come to mean anything that makes a big impact, such as a hit movie.

As with the term "blockbuster," *bombshell* for a beautiful woman comes from World War II and the many pinup girls of the time.

The term *cameo role*, which is a small part in a production, comes from the small but beautiful jewelry of the same name.

The word *fanny* used to describe the human backside comes from the 1749 book *Memoirs of a Woman of Pleasure* by John Cleland, also known as *Fanny Hill*. It is considered the first work of erotic prose in the English language.

A *ham* is someone who overdoes it while acting or showing off for the camera. The term comes from the days when minstrel performers wore black makeup on their faces and used ham fat to remove it.

> *Pulling strings* in order to get something done behind the scenes derives from the puppeteers of days gone by who controlled marionettes while out of sight.

A *blurb* is a short endorsement cited in promotional usage. The word comes from the fictional Miss Belinda Blurb. In 1907, humorist Gelett Burgess displayed a fake book jacket at a publishing convention featuring a beautiful woman with a brief "endorsement" from the fictitious Miss Blurb.

> In the 1500s, noblemen wore stockings and were quite concerned with the appearance of their legs and feet. At balls and other social functions they would stand with what they believed to be their more attractive foot forward, giving rise to the expression *best foot forward*.

Hanky-panky came into usage for a secret activity during the nineteenth-century when magicians would wave about a handkerchief with one hand to distract the audience from what they were doing with the other.

> Someone *on a high horse* feels superior to others. In days of yore, peasants rode mules, tradesmen rode horses, and the powerful rode great stallions.

To *read the riot act* is to rebuke and warn someone about his or her actions. The expression comes from English King George I, who issued a decree in 1716 that any time twelve or more people gathered to protest, officials would read them the act and disperse them.

> The word *tycoon* comes from the Chinese meaning "great prince."

Feather in one's cap comes from the time when warriors were given feathers to put in their hats for worthy deeds.

> *Wet behind the ears* can be traced to newly born animals that emerge wet from the womb. The area behind the ears is often the last to dry.

Break the ice comes from the icebreakers that needed to open a path for ships in northern European ports before they could get started during winter months.

> *Kingpin* comes from the early German bowling game ninepins, where one pin was taller than the rest—the king pin.

Getting one's ducks in a row harks back to early America when settlers played ten pins, a kind of bowling game. The pins were thought to resemble ducks and were called duckpins. They had to be arranged in rows before each frame was bowled.

Jackpot comes from draw poker, where a pair of jacks or better is required to open. Hands are dealt and antes are put into the pot until someone can open, often resulting in very large pots.

On a roll comes from the game of craps. Someone rolling a streak of winning dice throws was on a roll.

Start the ball rolling evolved from the game of croquet and the fact that the first person to go had the best chance of winning.

Cash on the barrelhead comes from early frontier saloons, where drinks might have been served on the top of a barrel in lieu of a bar proper. Patrons had to pay in advance by putting their cash on the barrelhead.

Gung ho is an expression used by the Chinese to synchronize the movements of workers on large projects. Early European visitors to China picked up on the expression and the enthusiasm it appeared to inspire in the workers.

Pipe dream came to mean a delusional idea during the late 1800s when England was flooded with opium from the Orient. Its smokers often had grand and confused thoughts.

Clip joint dates back to the time when coins were made of precious metals that could be shaved or clipped around the edges by unscrupulous merchants.

The addition of milled edges put an end to this practice.

Go haywire comes from a new hay-baling machine patented in 1828 by Moses Bliss. The contraption bound bales of hay in wire. Ofttimes the machine malfunctioned, tangling up workers and horses.

At *loose ends* comes from the practice on sailing ships for the crew to be given the busywork of securing/taping the loose ends of the numerous ropes on board when things were slow.

Make ends meet also comes from the sailing ships of old. Some sails had fixed ropes attached that had to be joined at the ends when they snapped. As the two halves got a little shorter in the process, this was accomplished with some difficulty.

A *pretty penny* is an expression rooted in the minting of a beautiful English gold piece in 1257 by Henry III. Its twenty-shilling value made it inconvenient for trade at the time, and it did not gain acceptance. As not many were minted, they became valuable, and people believed them to be good luck pieces.

Selling like hotcakes comes from the benefits put on by ladies' aid societies on the American frontier. They pan-fried corn hotcakes that were extremely popular and sold out quickly.

Blackball came into the language when clubs and societies held secret ballots to pick new members. Voting consisted of white balls for yes and black balls for no, which were placed in a hat. Often, just one black ball was enough to scuttle a candidate.

Boner, meaning mistake, comes from the idea that stupid people have heads full of bones, not brains.

Lay an egg comes from the inscrutable game of cricket where they say "you scored a duck's egg" if no points are scored.

Pull a fast one comes from baseball in the 1920s, when to get himself out of a jam a pitcher would suddenly throw a pitch of much greater velocity than he had been throwing.

Roger came to mean "yes" and "I understand" from the British pilots of the Royal Air Force. In radio communications, instead of saying "received," they used the first letter of the word, "r," which was "roger" in the radio alphabet of the time.

Ballpark estimate comes from the early days of baseball, when team owners didn't announce the size of the crowd and sportswriters just had to make an estimate.

Skid row originated from the early logging industry in the United States. Logs were dragged out of the forest to the nearest road on paths lined with wooden skids. In adjoining towns, a street with run-down buildings was known as a skid row by the loggers.

Whole hog dates back to the time of the Crusaders, who noticed that the Muslims they encountered would not eat pork, but would use a pig's bristles for brushes and its skin for water containers. The Europeans wondered why they didn't go "whole hog" and enjoy its meat as well.

Go to pot arose from the practice of throwing leftover bones and meat bits into a pot for stew after the good meat was eaten.

Stool pigeons were tame birds or decoys that were tied to stools in hopes of luring other birds close enough to shoot. In a way, these stool pigeons betrayed their brethren.

Dead as a doornail is thought to have originated from the heavy metal knockers used to pound on metal plates nailed on doors.

Wisdom teeth come in when one reaches adulthood and presumably is wiser than in youth.

When the Transcontinental Railroad was being built, it went through vast stretches of uninhabited land. To service the workers on the line, railcars filled with prostitutes followed and came to be called *hell on wheels*.

Over a barrel is where people about to be whipped were tied in early America.

Orders at sea were given by sounding the boatswain's pipe. When sailors were to go belowdecks and retire for the evening, they were *piped down*.

Cloth made and dyed blue in Coventry, England, stayed colorfast, or true. Hence the expression *true blue* for steadfast.

In medieval times, cannon tubes were held together with metal staves, such as those used on a barrel. This is the origin of the term gun "barrel."

Occasion, accommodate, maintenance, fiery, embarrassed, restaurant, vacuum, separate, recommend, and yes, misspell, are some of the most commonly misspelled words.

ACKNOWLEDGMENTS

I wish to thank my editor, Jeanette Shaw, for overseeing this wonderful series of useless information that the world so desperately needs. Also, I'd like to thank copyeditor Rick Willett for so thoroughly checking the myriad facts in this book, and Sarah Romeo for designing such a "magical" cover. As always, many thanks to my *extraordinary* literary agent, Janet Rosen.

ABOUT THE AUTHOR

Don Voorhees is the author of eleven books of trivia. A New Jersey native, he lives near Bethlehem, Pennsylvania, with his wife, Lisa, and two children, Eric and Dana.

He is always on the lookout for those tidbits of not-so-important information that his readers crave.